Ch

Cultural and Historical Perspectives

Revolutionary France

Paul R. Hanson

BUTLER UNIVERSITY

Copley Publishing Group
Acton, Massachusetts 01720

Copyright © 1996 by Paul R. Hanson. All rights reserved
Printed in the United States of America

Third printing 1999

ISBN 0-87411-814-X

Permission in writing must be obtained from the publisher before any part of this work may be reproduced or transmitted in any form or by any means, electronic or mechanical, including photocopying and recording, or by any information storage or retrieval system.

CONTENTS

CHRONOLOGICAL TABLE	v

PART I: OLD REGIME FRANCE

INTRODUCTION	3
GEOGRAPHY	5
HISTORICAL BACKGROUND	11
OLD REGIME SOCIETY	15
SOCIAL CLASSES	19
OLD REGIME ECONOMY	27
OLD REGIME GOVERNMENT	31
RELIGION AND THE CLERGY	35
IDEOLOGICAL ORIGINS OF THE FRENCH REVOLUTION	39
CAUSES OF THE FRENCH REVOLUTION	49

PART II: THE FRENCH REVOLUTION

1789	59
CONSTITUTIONAL MONARCHY, 1789-1792	71
THE FALL OF THE MONARCHY	81
RADICAL REPUBLIC, 1792-1794	83
THE TERROR	87
REVOLUTIONARY SYMBOLISM	89
THE FALL OF ROBESPIERRE	93
THE DIRECTORY REGIME AND THE RISE OF NAPOLEON	95
LEGACY	101
WORKS CITED	103
INDEX	105

MAPS

MAP 1:	Physical Geography of France	6
MAP 2:	Provinces of France/Restraints on Absolutism	7
MAP 3:	Thirty Largest Towns in France	51
MAP 4:	Revolutionary Departments and Response to Civil Constitution of the Clergy	75
MAP 5:	Napoleonic Empire	98

All maps prepared by Colleen Baker

ILLUSTRATIONS AND CHARTS

| **FIGURE 1:** | Revolutionary Assignat | 72 |
| **CHART 1:** | Revolutionary Calendar | 91 |

CHRONOLOGICAL TABLE

February 22-May 12, 1787	Assembly of Notables
August 8, 1788	King convokes Estates General
September 25, 1788	Parlement of Paris issues ruling on Estates General
May 5, 1789	Opening of Estates General
June 17, 1789	Third Estate calls itself the National Assembly
June 20, 1789	Tennis Court Oath
July 11, 1789	Dismissal of Necker
July 14, 1789	Fall of the Bastille
July 20-August 6	The Great Fear
August 4, 1789	Constituent Assembly abolishes feudalism
August 26, 1789	Assembly votes the Declaration of the Rights of Man
October 5-6, 1789	Women of Paris march to Versailles
November 2, 1789	Church lands nationalized
July 12, 1790	Assembly votes the Civil Constitution of the Clergy
June 20-21, 1791	Flight to Varennes
September 30, 1791	Legislative Assembly convenes
April 20, 1792	France declares war on Austria
April 24, 1792	Rouget de Lisle composes "La Marseillaise"
June 20, 1792	Failed assault on Tuileries Palace

August 10, 1792	Invasion of Tuileries/Fall of the monarchy
September 2-6, 1792	Massacre of Paris prisoners
September 20, 1792	Victory at Valmy/National Convention convenes
September 21, 1792	Convention declares Republic
December 11, 1792	Trial of Louis XVI begins
January 21, 1793	Execution of Louis XVI
February 1, 1793	France declares war on Britain and Holland
March 7, 1793	France declares war on Spain
March 10, 1793	Vendée rebellion begins
April 5, 1793	Committee of Public Safety established
May 4, 1793	Grain "maximum" decreed
May 31-June 2, 1793	Parisian uprising ousts Girondin deputies
June-August 1793	Federalist revolts
July 13, 1793	Murder of Marat
July 26, 1793	Convention votes death penalty for hoarders
September 4-5, 1793	Uprising in Paris: Convention makes Terror "the order of the day"
September 17, 1793	Convention votes the Law of Suspects
September 29, 1793	National "maximum" fixed for prices and wages
October 5, 1793	Convention adopts new calendar
October-November 1793	De-Christianization campaign
February 4, 1794	Convention abolishes slavery in French colonies

Chronology

April 5, 1794	Execution of Danton and his supporters
May 7, 1794	Robespierre institutes the Cult of the Supreme Being
July 27, 1794	Fall of Robespierre
November 19, 1794	Government closes Jacobin Clubs
May 20-22, 1795	Government defeats last great Paris uprising
August 22, 1795	Convention votes Constitution of Year III
October 5, 1795	Napoleon suppresses royalist uprising in Paris
October 26, 1795	Directory regime replaces National Convention
May 26, 1797	Gracchus Babeuf condemned to death
May 19, 1798	Napoleon sails to Egypt
November 10, 1799	Napoleon's coup d'état
1801	Napoleon signs Concordat with the Catholic Church
December 2, 1804	Napoleon crowns himself Emperor
June-October 1812	Napoleon's Russia campaign
March 1814	Napoleon abdicates throne, retires to Elba
March 1815	Napoleon returns to France
June 18, 1815	Wellington defeats Napoleon at Waterloo

PART I:

OLD REGIME FRANCE

INTRODUCTION

Theme and emphasis shift somewhat as we begin the second semester of "Change and Tradition." We leave behind the ancient and early modern worlds and enter a "modern" world that should be much more familiar to us, because it is closer to our own experience. Our emphasis to this point has been on tradition, but Revolutionary France was a society that rejected tradition and idealized change. Whereas in the first semester we explored, at least in part, the degree to which any great tradition must allow for change in order to maintain its own vitality, in this unit we should ask to what degree revolutionary change must preserve an element of tradition in order to make itself viable.

1789 marks the end of the Old Regime in France. This in itself is of no small consequence—the French monarchy ruled the most powerful nation in Europe in the 18th century, and since the reign of Louis XIV (1643-1715) the palace at Versailles had symbolized the grandeur of absolute monarchy. French was the court language of all of Europe, including Russia, and French culture generally set the standard for the rest of the continent. France was the most populous nation in Europe, numbering roughly 25,000,000 inhabitants on the eve of the Revolution, and was arguably the most prosperous.

Before considering the Revolution itself, then, we must explore the nature of the Old Regime and pose the question of why this prosperous, influential country should have experienced the first great, social revolution in world history. In other words, there are two major focuses to our study. Why did a revolution happen in France? And what in fact was the French Revolution and its impact?

Our inquiry begins with a discussion of French geography, in particular France's physical geography and the French international position. We turn then to a section on Old Regime government and society, focusing on the absolute monarchy created by Louis XIV and the corporate society over which that monarchy ruled. A discussion of the nature of the French economy in the 18th century, and the relationship between the Catholic Church and the monarchical state, will complete our picture of Old Regime France. We must then introduce ourselves, if only in passing, to some of the great Enlightenment thinkers, who were critical both of absolute monarchy and the institution of the Church. Finally, this first section will conclude with a consideration of the causes of the French Revolution.

GEOGRAPHY

France in the 17th and 18th centuries was essentially a land power, not a sea power. Although France is bordered by the English Channel to the northwest, the Atlantic Ocean to the west, and the Mediterranean Sea to the south, the French kings did not turn outward to sea trade and naval conquest. Instead they concentrated, especially Louis XIV, upon consolidating French continental power against the Netherlands to the north, the Holy Roman Empire to the east, and Spain to the south.

Since the time of Charlemagne (742-814) the French kingdom had grown piecemeal, radiating out gradually from the geographical cradle—Paris and the Ile de France (see Map 1). Parts of France, particularly the provinces of Guyenne and Gascony, had at one time been controlled by the king of England, and independent princes ruled several of the other provinces, such as Brittany, Artois, and Burgundy. The Bourbon kings, and revolutionary leaders of the 1790s, strove to expand France to its "natural boundaries:" the Atlantic Ocean on the west, the English Channel to the north, the Rhine River on the east, and the Alps and Pyrenees mountains to the south. On the eve of the Revolution, the boundaries of the French kingdom approximated those of France today.

However, one could not really speak of a unified French nation at that time. The central provinces, the *pays d'élection*, had been fully incorporated into the French monarchy and were subject to monarchical law and taxation. But more distant provinces, the *pays d'état*, had agreed to accept royal authority only in exchange for certain privileges, such as tax exemptions, the preservation of autonomous courts, and the right to convene provincial assemblies (see Map 2). The *pays d'état*, which included Brittany, Flanders, Lorraine, Alsace, Franche-Comté,

Burgundy, Dauphiné, Provence, Languedoc, Roussillon, Comté de Foix, and Béarn, thus enjoyed an element of independence from the French crown.

MAP 1: Physical Geography of France

Linguistic disunity reinforced this element of administrative disunity, for the majority of the kingdom's subjects did not in fact speak French. We should not exaggerate this factor, however, since the educated elite of the country did generally converse in Parisian French. But the peasants of Brittany spoke Breton, those of the south spoke the *langue d'oc* (language of oc), and the people in the region of Marseille spoke Provençal.

Peasants in many other regions spoke a variety of local *patois*, or dialects, often mutually unintelligible.

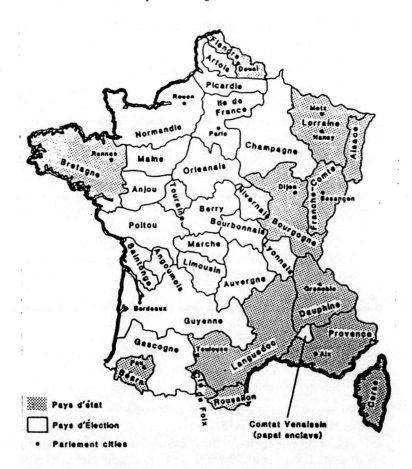

MAP 2: Provinces of France/ Restraints on Absolutism

Lest the reader be inclined to conclude from all this linguistic and administrative diversity that no such entity as France existed in the 18th century, let me offer some generalizations that allow us to think of France in terms of two parts rather than many. Historians and geographers have long been fond of telling their students that one can divide France by an imaginary line extending from St. Malo in the northwest to Geneva in the southeast. South of that line one found a Mediterranean culture. Wine and olives were widely cultivated on small, scattered farms; the legacy of the Roman empire had left a tradition of written law; literacy rates tended to be low; and rooftops were most commonly red tile. North of this imaginary line one encountered a northern European culture. Grain and cattle were produced on somewhat larger, commercial farms; a tradition of common law prevailed; literacy rates tended to be higher; and rooftops were more typically black slate. Traveling in France today, one still senses this general distinction between north and south.

Although France was a land power, water was not unimportant to the kingdom's economy. Three major rivers brought imported goods into the French interior and carried grain and wine downstream for export. The Rhône River, and its tributary the Saône, extended north from its mouth on the Mediterranean past Lyon, the European silk capital, into the heart of Burgundy. The Loire River, flanked by impressive châteaux, meandered through central and western France from its headwaters just south of Lyon to the Atlantic seaport of Nantes. The Garonne River connected the heartland of the southwest to Bordeaux and the Gironde estuary. Finally, the Seine River carried goods upstream from the ports of Le Havre and Rouen to the capital, Paris.

Overseas France could not equal the maritime powers England and the Netherlands, or Spain and Portugal in an earlier era, yet France was active in commercial trade and colonial expansion. The port of Marseille imported grain from Turkey, the Middle East, and North Africa, while exporting wine, silk, and other luxury goods. Bordeaux, La Rochelle and Nantes all participated in the active Atlantic trade, carrying slaves from Africa to the West Indies and returning with spices, tobacco and sugar. By the early 18th century France possessed a sizable colonial empire, ranging from North America and the Caribbean islands in the West to India in the East. That empire was shattered, however, by the Seven Years' War (1756-1763) between France and Great Britain. France lost its North American and Indian holdings to the British, and saw her influence in the Caribbean much diminished as well.

HISTORICAL BACKGROUND

French civilization has its roots in classical antiquity. Greek colonists founded Marseille in the 6th century B.C., and Julius Caesar conquered all of France (then known as Gaul) for the Romans five centuries later. The Romans left behind not only a legacy of written law, but a number of impressive structures, including the Pont du Gard aqueduct and the amphitheater of Nimes in southern France. During the French Revolution, legislators strove to reclaim the republican and democratic traditions of Rome and Greece as well.

French dynastic history began with the Carolingian dynasty, consolidated by Charlemagne, and continued under the Capetian dynasty, whose final branch was the Bourbon royal family, beginning with Henri IV in 1589 and ending finally with Louis-Philippe in 1848. We will be concerned chiefly with two Bourbon kings: Louis XIV, who epitomized the tradition of absolute monarchy; and Louis XVI, whose reign ended on the guillotine in January 1793.

The reign of Louis XIV (1643-1715) was characterized both by grandeur and catastrophe. Louis was only five years old when he ascended the throne, and he ruled with the able assistance of his first minister, Cardinal Mazarin, until 1661. His authority was challenged early by the Fronde (1648-1653), a rebellion led by powerful nobles intent upon recovering their regional power, which they had lost early in the century to the centralizing policies of Louis XIII and his first minister, Cardinal Richelieu. The Fronde ultimately failed, but the revolt terrified the young king and left him determined to strengthen the power of the monarchy.

Louis began that task in earnest in 1661, the year that Mazarin died, leaving Louis to assume full control over the reins of power. Louis XIV was a man of exceptional determination and energy. He had an extraordinary appetite for work, as well as for food and drink. Louis' endurance at royal feasts was legendary, a capacity made possible, as was ultimately shown at his autopsy, by a stomach four times the size of a normal man's. Whether or not he ever in fact uttered the famous words, "L'état c'est moi" (I am the state), his actions and policies certainly suggested a belief in such a maxim.

After the death of Mazarin, Louis abandoned the practice of his father and ruled without a first minister. The ministers in his Council of State served at his whim, and the king thus dominated affairs of state, dependent on no single official. Otherwise he continued the centralizing policies of his father and did much to create a bureaucratic administration. The most important elements in that administration were the Intendants, the king's representatives in the provinces. These men did not buy their offices, as was true of many other Old Regime officials, but rather were appointed by the king, and Louis XIV made a point of choosing men of bourgeois origins, rather than nobles, to serve as his Intendants. He also assigned the Intendants (whose numbers ranged from 30 to 35 over time) to posts away from their home provinces, in order to prevent them from establishing a local power base that might undermine the authority of the monarchy.

Louis' efforts to strengthen royal power and weaken the provincial nobility manifested themselves in a more dramatic fashion as well. During the final fifty years of his reign (which extended seventy-two years!), Louis XIV devoted great energy, and expense, to the construction of the dazzling palace at Versailles. Built on the site of a royal hunting lodge some ten miles south of Paris, Versailles reflected the grandeur of Louis, the Sun King, and the splendour of French culture. Peter the Great of Russia and Frederick the Great of Prussia each built palaces modeled upon Versailles. The palace's numerous wings, designed by the architects Le Vau and Le Nôtre, were decorated by the paintings and tapestries of Le Brun and the sculpture of Bernini, Coysevox, and Rigaud. Beyond the buildings the gardens of Le Nôtre extended three miles, emulating for public view both the rationality of Louis' kingdom and the control of man over nature. In these elegant gardens and stately rooms the music of Lully and the plays of Molière added to the glitter and glory of Louis' monarchy.

More than a reflection of Louis' greatness, Versailles was a tool in his centralizing policy. In the past the king of France and the royal court had traveled widely in the kingdom, visiting the king's domains and the provincial châteaux of powerful nobles. Louis XIV ruled from Versailles, and those nobles who sought royal favor had to live at Versailles for much of the year. To be sure, they were lavishly entertained by a seemingly continuous festival of music and theatre, but to decline the king's generosity was to risk the ruin of one's reputation, and possibly one's fortune. Those most favored by Louis were privileged to visit his bedchamber each morning to witness the ceremonial dressing of the king. In this manner Louis separated the realm's powerful nobles from their provincial strongholds and made them, ritually and literally, his servants.

Louis XIV also succeeded in undermining the power of the thirteen provincial *parlements* in France. These independent courts, principally composed of prominent nobility who had purchased their offices, had traditionally acted as a restraint upon royal despotism. The *parlement* of Paris, the most powerful among them, had to register all royal edicts before they became law. Under Louis XIV, and until the 1750s, that registration became virtually automatic.

By 1685 Louis XIV had created a royal bureaucracy whose officials were beholden to him, had tamed the old aristocracy in its provincial seats and the *parlements,* and had built a magnificent palace at Versailles that epitomized the absolute monarchy embodied in the person of the Sun King. Under the steady hand of his finance minister, Jean Baptiste Colbert, the administrative machinery of the state functioned smoothly and provided the king with the revenues needed for his lavish building projects and expensive wars. Louis XIV fancied himself a military hero, and in the 1660s and 1670s his armies conquered significant territories along the northern and eastern borders, including Alsace and Lorraine. Louis' ambition was to dominate Europe, and from 1685 to the end of his reign France was almost constantly at war. Those three decades brought few decisive victories, however, and fewer gains. Finally, in the War of the Spanish Succession (1701-1713), the English, Dutch, Austrians, and Prussians combined in the Grand Alliance to prevent Louis from joining Spain and the Spanish Netherlands to the French crown. The constant wars had disrupted the French economy and overtaxed the peasantry, leaving the kingdom in a weakened, even miserable, state at the end of Louis XIV's reign. The expulsion of the Huguenots (French Protestants) in 1685 had weakened the economy (many Huguenots were merchants or artisans) and deepened religious divisions. The nadir came in 1709, when a crippling freeze left much of the country literally with no harvest. Tens of thousands died of cold, starvation or disease in 1709-1710, in the last great demographic crisis of the Old Regime. Although Louis' reign had been a glorious one, it did not always redound to the glory, or the benefit, of his people.

OLD REGIME SOCIETY

If we are to understand the Revolution that itself introduced the term "old regime," then we must first know something about the society that produced that revolution. Two concepts may be helpful to us in understanding the way that society was organized. The first of these is the "Great Chain of Being" and the related idea of estates. According to this concept, prevalent since medieval times, the entire world was organized hierarchically, extending from God and the angels at the top to inanimate objects such as rocks at the bottom. Human beings, of course, fell somewhere in between. Every creature or thing in this chain was in some sense linked to those immediately above and below on the ladder. We can easily sense the difference between people and cows (although Diderot did once write that it would be difficult to precisely *define* the difference between d'Alembert and a cow), but we can also discern similarities. Moreover, particularly within the human population, those higher on the chain had a certain responsibility to those below, while those in the lower ranks owed deference and obedience to those above. At the top of the human chain stood the king, while at the bottom one found the lowliest vagrant or thief.

Compatible with this hierarchical Chain of Being was the idea of "estates" or "orders." Old regime society was legally divided into three estates, again hierarchically arranged. The First Estate, the clergy, enjoyed that status by virtue of its spiritual function and proximity to God. The clergy comprised no more than one percent of the population. The Second Estate, the nobility, enjoyed its status by virtue of military service rendered to the king. Many nobles, or aristocrats (the terms are virtually synonymous), could trace their lineage back to the knights of the Middle Ages, some to the time of Charlemagne. Nobility was defined by blood—one was born into a noble family. Since 1600 French monarchs had occasionally sold noble titles to raise money for their wars, or had granted nobility to those men who served as officials in the royal administration. This latter group is often referred to as "robe nobility," as opposed to the older "sword nobility." By 1789 the distinction between the two had become relatively meaningless, but traditionally the "sword nobility" looked down upon the recently ennobled "robe nobility." The nobility, including family members, numbered perhaps 400,000 people, from one to two percent of the population. The Third Estate, the remaining ninety-seven percent of the population, comprised everyone else: professionals (lawyers, teachers, doctors), bourgeois (merchants, bankers, shop owners), workers, peasants, beggars, and vagrants. We must bear in mind that France was an overwhelmingly rural society, and the peasantry itself represented roughly eighty-five percent of the population.

The second useful concept in thinking about Old Regime society is that of "corporatism," and the accompanying idea of "privilege." Old Regime society consisted of a number of overlapping "corporate" bodies, each possessing certain privileges (from the Latin *privi legis*, or private law) particular to it. This is a somewhat difficult concept, given that it has very little to do with our modern notions of a corporate society. Some examples may be helpful. Each of the three estates could be thought of as a corporate body, although in everyday life the unity of any one of them might not have been apparent. More obvious to 18th-century French people would have been the corporate guilds. Virtually every urban craftsman belonged to a guild, such as that of the hatmakers, the goldsmiths, the ironworkers, the carpenters, the shoemakers, etc. These guilds, like the rest of society, were organized hierarchically. One entered as an apprentice, became a journeyman as one learned certain skills, and, with a measure of talent and luck, ended one's career as a master craftsman. Each guild enjoyed certain legal privileges (with regard to taxes, the selling of goods, and occasionally elections) and a place in the urban hierarchy, reflected on holidays by the position of guild members in the local parades. The guild controlled entry into the trade, and one could not produce or sell goods in a town unless one belonged to the appropriate guild. In addition to the privileges guild members enjoyed, the guilds functioned as a means for the monarchy to control the trades, by limiting numbers and policing standards of quality.

Chartered towns are another example of a corporate body enjoying certain privileges, and every inhabitant of such a town was, in a sense, privileged. Chartered towns (such as Lille, in northern France, added to the realm during the reign of Louis XIV) might enjoy tax exemptions, exemption from various commercial duties, and the privilege of electing a municipal council. Indeed, in comparison to the countryside nearly every town was privileged in some sense. Many enjoyed tax exemptions of one sort or another (to encourage trade and business), and the king granted many others the privilege of holding seasonal fairs.

As two final examples of corporate bodies we might mention the *parlements*, the high courts whose members enjoyed exalted status, and often the privilege of passing their position on to their sons; and also the *pays d'état*, those privileged provinces most recently incorporated into the kingdom. The principal point to be made here is that a person living in 18th-century France did not define himself or herself as an individual citizen enjoying certain inalienable rights. Rather, each person thought of himself or herself as a subject of the king, enjoying various privileges by virtue of his or her membership in one or more corporate bodies. One identified oneself by one's family, one's guild, one's town, one's province, etc.

We can thus think of Old Regime France as a particularistic society composed of privileged estates and corporate bodies. Our tendency to think of the nobility and the clergy as the privileged members of French society is misleading, as we have seen. Virtually everyone enjoyed privileges of one sort or another, depending on the groups to which they belonged. What at first glance appears to be an orderly, traditional society, simple in structure compared to our own, was in fact very complex. Indeed, the French historian Pierre Goubert has written that "the quintessence of the *ancien regime* is confusion...." (Goubert, 17). Even Goubert, however, tries to generalize with caution, and we shall do the same as we turn to consider the social classes that made up French society.

SOCIAL CLASSES

The clergy may have been the First Estate, but it was the nobility that stood at the top of French society in terms of social status. We have already noted the distinction between "sword" and "robe" nobility, but even within those two categories there are further distinctions. The wealthiest and most powerful of the Old Regime nobles, numbering perhaps a few hundred families, were known as *Les Grands*. These were the oldest noble families in France, their aristocratic lineage dating back centuries. They owned large landholdings, generally scattered over several provinces, and lived in elegant châteaux, moving from one to another depending on the season. Most of *Les Grands* also maintained a *hôtel* (town house) in Paris, the center of French social and cultural life. Living off the income from their land and investments, *Les Grands* enjoyed an elegant, even luxurious, lifestyle. Traditionally they claimed a considerable political influence, as councillors of state and *parlement* judges, but under Louis XIV their power had waned. Under the weaker reigns of Louis XV and Louis XVI the influence of *Les Grands* increased once again.

Just below *Les Grands* in status came a group we might call the parliamentary nobility, also numbering several hundred families. These men sat as judges in one of the thirteen *parlements* in France. In the Paris *parlement* the noble status of some of these men was occasionally of recent origin, but in the provinces this was rarely the case. By the second half of the 18th century virtually all of the *parlementaires* were nobles of long standing.

Provincial nobles constituted a third identifiable segment of the nobility, and these we must separate into two groups. The first lived very comfortably, though on a more modest scale than *Les Grands*. They typically kept both a country estate and a hotel in a provincial town, but did not spend extended periods in Paris and made no pretensions to a role in national affairs. Many of these nobles were *seigneurs* (lords of the manor), with scores of peasants working their lands under various sorts of rental agreements, and most held the privilege of sitting as judge over their own local court (as did Count Almaviva in *The Marriage of Figaro*). The second group, known as *hobereaux*, were old noble families that had fallen on hard times. Traditionally the nobility was forbidden to engage in commerce or industry, at the risk of losing their noble status (a penalty known as *dérogeance*). The opulent lifestyle that most nobles felt obliged to maintain could quickly deplete a family fortune. Such was the case for the *hobereaux*, country gentlemen living in genteel poverty, in some cases able to keep only a servant or two and reduced to heating only a few rooms of their large and once bustling households. They preserved their noble status and the honorific privileges that accompanied it (the right to wear a sword, a special pew at church, etc.), but their days of glory lay in the past.

We must finally mention the new nobility, those "robe" nobility who had acquired that rank through service in the royal bureaucracy or by special edict of the king. To some degree this constituted simply a replenishment of the ranks of the nobility, since old family lineages became extinct at the rate of 20 to 30 percent each century (Goubert, 179). On the other hand, Louis XIV clearly used ennoblement of commoners as a means to undermine the power of the old nobility.

One might achieve noble status by two routes. The first was by a letter of ennoblement, a favor that French kings had bestowed upon deserving subjects (generally no more than 5-10 per year) since the 14th century. This conferral of noble status was in part a fundraising device—the recipients of this honor responded with a modest donation to the crown.

The second means of achieving noble status, the purchase of certain royal offices, was even more blatantly a fundraising device for the monarchy. Some royal positions, such as that of *secrétaire du roi*, conferred immediate nobility upon the purchaser. By the end of the Old Regime the cost of this office had reached 300,000 *livres*, the price of a substantial town house (Goubert, 183). Other less costly offices conferred nobility only if held by the same family over two or three generations. After 1604 such noble status became inheritable. The monarchy sold both administrative and judicial offices, with nobility attached, to raise funds for the treasury. Some contemporaries argued that the sale of judicial offices assured an independent judiciary, and thus created a check on royal power. Others, such as the playwright Beaumarchais, pilloried venality of offices as one of the most corrupt practices of the Old Regime.

The nobility, then, was a relatively varied social group. What united the nobility was a shared sense of honor (nobles possessed this, no one else did) and an array of honorific privileges. We have noted that a nobleman might lose his status for engaging in business or trade, but the splendid isolation of the nobility should not be exaggerated. New money constantly came into the nobility, as merchants and industrialists purchased ennobling offices to cap a successful career, and it was not uncommon for the son of a noble to take a bourgeois bride, who would of course contribute a large dowry to the marriage. As Madame de Sévigné once remarked in reference to her bourgeois daughter-in-law: "Even the most cultivated land can use a little manure."

By the 18th century it was also not uncommon for an industrialist or overseas merchant to continue his business after his purchase of noble office. Many historians have recently argued that on the eve of the Revolution it is very difficult to distinguish wealthy nobles from wealthy bourgeois. Certainly the social and economic differences between the two groups had diminished. Legally, however, the nobility remained a distinctly separate order.

Just below the nobility on the social hierarchy we find the bourgeoisie, a term sometimes rendered in English as the middle class. The bourgeoisie of the 18th century, however, was not the equivalent of the modern middle class. Dating back to medieval times, "bourgeois" was a legal category, denoting an individual who lived permanently in town (a bourg), who owned his house, and who met certain other requirements, which varied from town to town. These men typically lived off their investments, either in land, government bonds, or loans.

From the early 17th century onward, as the size of the royal bureaucracy grew, we see a growing number of bourgeois officials. These ranged from low-level clerks and secretaries in provincial offices to high-ranking administrative and judicial officials who might one day hope to achieve noble status. They owed their social position, quite literally, to the monarchy.

It is in the 18th century that we see a rather dramatic increase in the commercial and industrial bourgeoisie. The big merchants of the Atlantic seaports were among the wealthiest men in France, and through much of the 18th century their fortunes prospered. The manufacturing bourgeoisie was more modest in scale and number. The more prosperous manufacturers also tended to be involved in commerce. Linked to the wholesale merchants of the large ports were the hundreds of small merchants and shopkeepers so typical of the French commercial economy—the *petite bourgeoisie*.

Until the end of the Old Regime the most socially respectable form of wealth remained landed wealth. It was common, then, for the bourgeoisie, no matter how they earned their money, to eventually invest it in land. Sometimes they moved to the countryside to oversee their new estates, but often they remained absentee landlords who hired managers to run their affairs. Some became *seigneurs*, having purchased a *seigneurie* that required the resident peasants to deliver dues and services to the landowner, whether he be noble or commoner. This "rural bourgeoisie" led a modest trend toward commercial agriculture, which often aroused resentment and resistance among the tradition-minded peasantry.

Just below the bourgeoisie on the urban social scale we encounter what may be called, for lack of a more precise label, the lower classes, what the French called *le menu peuple* (the little people), or more pejoratively *la canaille* (the rabble). There was no such cohesive social group as "the working class," a term that is really not appropriate until the 19th century. The urban lower classes in France were a combination of skilled and semi-skilled artisans employed by master craftsmen who paid them a piece-rate for their work; a vast array of unskilled workers who performed menial labor, acted as messengers, porters, errand boys, etc.; women and children employed in specialized branches of the textile industry (silk and lace in particular) and who were paid a modest piece-rate, less than male workers; and finally a relatively small number of wage earners—the seeds of a modern working class—employed for an hourly wage in textile mills, in other factory production, and on the docks of seaports. Like the nobility and the bourgeoisie, then, this was a diverse group with no real class consciousness, linked to the upper classes more by patron-client ties than by feelings of class resentment. To the extent that these people shared common grievances, they were motivated more by consumer concerns (the price of bread) than by a desire for higher wages.

In the countryside we find the peasantry at the lower end of the social scale. Remember that France remained an overwhelmingly rural society at the end of the Old Regime, and that the peasantry comprised perhaps 85 percent of the population, among which, as in the other social groups, we encounter great diversity.

Alexis de Tocqueville observed long ago that the French peasantry was relatively prosperous, certainly the most prosperous on the European continent, and his observation has endured the test of time. It is difficult to estimate the number of peasants who owned their own land, but certainly it was no more than 40 percent and perhaps substantially less. Many landowning peasants, moreover, did not own enough land to adequately support their families. Some rented land to supplement their own parcel, while others engaged in a rural handicraft that brought in additional income. Still others hired themselves out as laborers during peak agricultural seasons. Overall, far fewer than 40 percent could be called truly independent peasants.

The majority of peasants rented their land, either as tenant farmers (*fermiers à bail*) or as sharecroppers (*métayers*). There were countless types of contract or arrangement that tied these dependent peasants to their landlords, far too many to chronicle here. Some rented land in a straight lease arrangement, generally with a long-term lease. Some worked the land of a lord, and delivered to him both rent and services. Others could be characterized as sharecroppers, peasants who shared the harvest proportionally with the owner of the land. Finally, there were a great many peasants, their number fluctuating from year to year, who neither owned nor rented land, but hired themselves out as day laborers.

During hard years of poor harvest, such as those on the eve of the Revolution, thousands fell from the ranks of the respectable peasantry into the ranks of vagrants and beggars. They would take to the road, wandering the countryside in search of alms or something to steal. Those who failed in their search starved, froze, or succumbed to disease. Life for most was short and precarious in 18th-century France. Returning to Tocqueville's observation, we must emphasize that the French peasantry was only *relatively* prosperous.

One thing that marked the French peasant apart from most others on the continent was that serfdom had largely disappeared from France between the 14th and 16th centuries. Many peasants were not completely independent, and most tended to remain in the village or province of their parents, but they were not bound to the land they worked. Vestiges of serfdom did persist in 18th-century France, and these are generally referred to as comprising the seigneurial system. The system was not uniform across France, and in characterizing it we might recall the north/south dichotomy mentioned earlier. In northern France, the old saying went, there was "no land without lord," whereas in southern France there existed "no lord without title" (Goubert, 85). Seigneurialism survived, quite widely, by tradition in the north, while seigneurial dues could only be collected by virtue of legal title in the south. Most seigneurs (lords) were noblemen, but not all—a bourgeois could purchase a seigneurial estate and title. Seigneurial obligations were harshest in the provinces of Burgundy and Brittany, where the practice of *mainmorte* (mortmain, from the Latin for "dead hand") still survived. Peasants holding land under *mainmorte* could not legally leave the land, and if they failed to bear children the property reverted to the lord upon death. Peasants in this situation were very nearly serfs.

In other provinces the dues and services owed by peasants were less severe. Peasants who worked land (either owned or rented) on a seigneurial domain might be required to work a certain number of days a year on the lord's land; grind their grain in the lord's mill; press their grapes in the lord's press; or bake their bread in the lord's oven (in each case the lord would receive a portion of grain, wine, or bread). Often the peasant owed to the lord a portion of his crop, or might periodically be required to deliver to the lord a chicken or some eggs. In some areas the dues and duties were light, and in others onerous. Some seigneurs were benevolent, others were harsh. In all cases, the benefits that the peasants received in exchange—protection from bandits and rival princes in feudal times—had largely disappeared by the 18th century, and the seigneurial system was widely resented by the peasantry.

Most peasants were subject to another payment (in addition to taxes, to be discussed below) that cut into the amount of the harvest available for their own use. This was the tithe. The tithe was in theory a gift to the church, collected from producers, not landowners, immediately after the harvest. The tithe was paid in kind, that is a portion of the harvest went to the tithe owner. The tithe varied from one region to the next, though it rarely equalled the ten percent that we commonly associate with tithing. In theory the tithe went to support the parish priest and the poor, but in practice the right to collect the tithe was often owned by monastic orders, or even secular individuals, whose relation to the local population in spiritual matters was indirect or nonexistent. Peasants increasingly resented this payment, which they viewed as benefitting the wealthy rather than the needy.

OLD REGIME ECONOMY

We have already touched upon aspects of the economy in our discussion of the seigneurial system and the status of the peasantry. It was predominantly a rural, agricultural economy, employing traditional methods and governed by local needs and local conditions. The vestiges of feudalism—not only seigneurial dues, but also community traditions regarding crop rotation, fallow land, and the right to graze animals on common land—tended to preserve subsistence farming and impede the emergence of commercial agriculture. Unlike England, there was no dramatic enclosure movement in Old Regime France, and small landholdings remained the norm well into the 20th century. Peasants typically grew grain—wheat, rye, oats or barley, depending on the region—and a small plot of vegetables. In Burgundy, Languedoc, and Guyenne wine production complemented the cultivation of local grains. Along the Mediterranean coast olives were an important crop.

Subsistence farming dominated French agriculture under the Old Regime. Peasants produced primarily for their own needs. Whatever surplus they might produce was quickly absorbed by rents, tithes, seigneurial dues, and taxes. Those lucky enough to have grain or vegetables to sell did so locally, at regional markets and fairs. France was not blessed, like England, with an extensive network of rivers and canals. Grain barges did move up the Rhône, Loire, and Seine rivers, to be sure, but much of the French population lived far away from waterways. France did possess a superb network of royal highways, the best roads in all of Europe, and it was expanded and improved after 1750. But travel by road was expenseive, slow (it took five days, at least, to travel by coach from Paris to Marseille), and often impossible during the winter. The expense of transportation, in particular, prevented the development of a truly national market in France until well into the 19th century. Provincial tariff barriers and the lack of a national currency or system of weights and measures further impeded trade. Only the large towns and cities pulled grain supplies from distant sources.

Alongside this traditional agricultural sector, however, commercial trade was expanding in the 17th and 18th centuries, encouraged by royal policy. Louis XIV's controller-general, Jean Baptiste Colbert, formulated a mercantilist policy in the second half of the 17th century. Mercantilist theory held that the wealth of a nation could best be increased by the accumulation of precious metals, e.g. gold and silver. If a country did not own mines (as did Spain, in its New World possessions), then the only means to accumulate precious metals lay in trade. Not only should the monarchy encourage trade, argued Colbert, it should control it. Thus, the East India Companies of France and England, which monopolized each nation's trade with India, were creations of mercantilist policy. Under Colbert this policy extended beyond international trade to the manufacturing sector. Before a nation can grow rich through trade, it must have something to trade. The monarchy therefore encouraged manufacturing (the Gobelins tapestry works is a good example) and France developed an international reputation for the production of luxury goods (silk, satin, lace, perfumes, etc.). In order to regulate manufacturing and commerce, the monarchy fostered the creation of corporate guilds. The king granted the guilds the privilege of producing or selling certain goods, and the guilds reported regularly to royal inspectors. In this fashion standards of quality were maintained and competition was controlled. To secure access to raw materials, and tap new markets, Colbert also encouraged colonial expansion. One can dispute the wisdom of Colbert's policies, but during his tenure in office and for some years thereafter the growth in French trade brought prosperity to ports such as Lyon, Marseille, Bordeaux, La Rochelle, Nantes, Le Havre, and Paris itself.

In the second half of the 18th century, however, a group of thinkers known as the Physiocrats, or Economists, challenged Colbert's mercantilism. Led by François Quesnay, they argued that the only true source of wealth was agriculture, since only agriculture truly created a product from nothing. Trade obviously created nothing, it only exchanged things, and manufacturing really only transformed things into something else. Far from encouraging agricultural production, however, the monarchy actually fettered it by controlling grain prices and imposing excessive taxes on the peasantry. The Physiocrats advocated free trade in grain and policies designed to encourage agricultural production. The monarchy did introduce free trade in grain on two occasions, but in each case poor harvests and peasant riots forced the reimposition of controls. Not until the Revolution was the physiocratic program, similar in many ways to the theories of Adam Smith, more fully introduced.

OLD REGIME GOVERNMENT

We have already encountered some elements of Old Regime government in our discussion of Louis XIV's centralizing policies. In a simplistic sense, the history of the monarchy in the 17th century is the story of its power increasing as that of the old nobility declined. Although the king obviously could not govern alone, in theory he ruled as absolute monarch, God's divine representative. Nowhere is this better expressed than in this 1766 proclamation of Louis XV:

> Sovereign power resides in my person alone.... It is from me alone that my policies take their existence and their authority; ... it is to me alone that legislative power belongs, without dependence or division; ... all public order emanates from me.
> (Miller, 120)

The king may have been an absolute monarch in theory, but not even in theory was he omnipotent or omnipresent. To assist the king in governing the country a bureaucratic administration developed over time—not a rationally organized bureaucracy, but rather the product of pragmatic responses to existing needs. It came into existence piecemeal, beginning in the reign of Louis XIII and largely in place at the death of Louis XIV. Without attempting an exhaustive description, we can at least identify its most important features.

At the top of the bureaucracy stood the council of state, composed of a handful of ministers who served on the council at the king's invitation. This group advised the king on the most important policy matters. Even at this level we see an inherent structural tension. Louis XIV made membership on the council of state by invitation so that he could more easily dominate decisions of state and control his ministers. Under the weaker monarchs who succeeded him, this instability meant that ministers competed for the king's favor, often undermining each others' policies in their desire to secure a favored position. At its worst, this infighting produced vacillating and contradictory government policy.

Below the council of state, two other bodies assisted the king in governing France: the council of dispatches, composed of all the most important royal officials, which governed internal policy; and the Privy Council, which managed the administration of the kingdom, but did not set policy. Eighty masters of requests served as liaisons between the Privy Council and the king's most important representatives in the provinces, the Intendants. The Intendants, however, were not assigned to the traditional provinces. Instead the monarchy created new administrative districts, the generalities, to which the thirty-four Intendants were dispatched. The boundaries of the generalities were not the same as the provincial boundaries, nor were they the same as the boundaries of judicial districts. Royal administration, obviously, was not entirely rational.

At this level we see another of the tensions that plagued Old Regime government. In creating new administrative structures Louis XIV did not eliminate, but rather simply ignored, the structures they replaced. Thus provincial governors continued as supreme military commanders in the provinces, and in other ways competed with the authority of the intendants. The governors tended to be prominent nobles, evidence that Louis XIV's determination to break the power of the nobility had fallen short of its goal.

The authority of the Intendants was further limited by the existence of provincial estates in the three most important *pays d'état*—Brittany, Languedoc, and Burgundy. These estates were not elected bodies, but they did claim to be representative of their provinces in a certain sense and reserved the right to register royal taxes and other important legislation.

The Intendants also occasionally clashed with the thirteen provincial *parlements* (located in Paris, Rennes, Rouen, Douai, Metz, Nancy, Besançon, Dijon, Grenoble, Aix, Toulouse, Bordeaux, and Pau). These were not legislative bodies, but rather were the most important judicial courts of the kingdom. In addition to that function, they traditionally registered all royal legislation before it became law. Legislation opposed by a *parlement* could be protested to the king by a private "remonstrance," which the king could override by issuing a *lit de justice* ("bed of justice," a forced registration). Louis XIV had succeeded in subduing the *parlements*, but they revived in the 18th century and, led by the *parlement* of Paris, increasingly claimed to represent the nation in opposition to what they perceived as monarchical despotism.

Supporting this complicated administrative structure was a system of taxation that was at least as confusing, and arguably less efficient. Frenchmen paid a combination of direct and indirect taxes, and overall these taxes weighed most heavily upon the poorest of the crown's subjects, the peasantry. The principal direct taxes were the *taille*, the *vingtième*, and the *capitation*. The major tax, the *taille*, was levied as a personal tax in the north and as a land tax in the south. It bore no consistent relation to personal income, however, since the *taille* was assessed as a lump sum to the provinces, districts, and then parishes. In each parish or village a peasant would be designated to levy and collect the tax quota. In theory the nobility was exempt from the *taille*, but in the south nobles did pay tax on their common lands, generally a sizable portion of their holdings. The *vingtième* (twentieth tax), introduced as a modest tax on income in 1749 at the end of the War of Austrian Succession, was doubled and then tripled during the Seven Years' War. The French viewed the *vingtième* as a special war tax, and greatly resented it when it persisted into the 1780s, a decade of peace. The *capitation* was a hearth tax (household tax) levied on all Frenchmen, nobility included, that varied according to social position (there were twenty-two classifications). In theory the very poor did not pay the *capitation*.

A variety of indirect taxes supplemented the direct taxes. These included tariffs, excise taxes, and sales taxes, and they varied enormously from one province to the next. Some provinces (principally the *pays d'état*) were entirely exempt from certain taxes. The most onerous and hated of these taxes was the *gabelle*, or salt tax. Salt was of course a necessity in the 18th century—meat could not be preserved without it—and in many areas the *gabelle* mandated that families purchase a minimum amount of salt. The indirect taxes were collected by "tax farmers." Each year the Farmers General (*Fermiers Généraux*) contracted with the monarchy to collect indirect taxes and guarantee an overall revenue to the crown. In bad years the crown benefited from this arrangement because the tax farmers had to absorb any deficit, but in good years the tax farmers made out like bandits, sometimes collecting twice the revenue they had promised to the king. Successful tax farmers were among the wealthiest, and most hated, people in France.

This complicated tax system was both inefficient and unfair. Privileged individuals, towns, and even entire provinces, were exempt from certain taxes. It is an exaggeration to suggest that the nobility were entirely exempt—most paid the *capitation* and many paid the *taille*. But certainly it is true that the peasantry paid more than its fair share. Although it is difficult to calculate a precise figure, in some areas of France the peasant farmer appears to have paid direct taxes equal to 50 to 60 percent of his gross harvest. Given that a fifth to a quarter of the harvest had to be saved for seed for the following year, this left very little grain for the family to consume. By the end of the Old Regime this burdensome tax system was the focus of great resentment, much of it directed against the one group that was virtually exempt from all direct taxes—the clergy.

RELIGION AND THE CLERGY

The vast majority of people in Old Regime France professed Catholicism as their religion. On the eve of the Revolution there were perhaps 700,000 Protestants and 30,000 Jews in France, living amidst 24,000,000 Catholics. Between Catholics and Protestants there had been considerable hostility in the past. Henri IV had granted religious toleration to Protestants by his 1598 Edict of Nantes, thereby ending a generation of religious warfare. In 1685, however, Louis XIV revoked that edict and many French Protestants, known as Huguenots, fled the kingdom. Those who remained in France could not openly practice their faith until 1787, when Louis XVI issued another decree of toleration. French Jews, fewer in number and relatively dispersed geographically, were not overtly persecuted under the Old Regime, although certainly they experienced social and economic discrimination.

We must think of Catholicism both as a religion and as an important institution in Old Regime France. Religion pervaded daily life in the 18th century. There was less emphasis upon overt religiosity than in 15th-16th century Spain—one did not have to prove one's Catholicity on a regular basis—but in other respects we find clear similarities. Mass and devotional services were the most important social, as well as religious, events in most towns and villages. Religious holidays and saints' days sprinkled the calendar with a variety of festivals, large and small, that provided a respite from work. Those without work turned to the Church as the principal source of charity. Nearly every village and town claimed the protection of a patron saint. Those who attended school were taught by priests of the Jesuit Order, which was founded by the Spaniard Ignatius Loyola. Parents gave their children religious names—Marie and Jean-Baptiste were extremely popular in the 18th century. We should be aware, however, that religiosity and superstition are often difficult to distinguish in this period. Catholicism did not encourage the reading of the Bible, as did Protestantism, so that most individuals were not well versed in the Scriptures. For peasants, their relationship to God, or the Virgin Mary, was essentially contractual. Regular devotions and prayer were expected to bring good health and plentiful harvests, at the very least to protect them from crisis and disaster. Many peasants believed that the images of saints themselves possessed magical powers—that a statue of Saint Barbara, for example, was a *real* image, not a symbolic one, and that by touching it one would be blessed. Catholicism exercised a pervasive influence in Old Regime society—it defined the world view of most people—but to say that much is only to begin to understand the complexity of the Catholic religion in this period.

It is easier to understand the role of the Catholic Church as an institution in Old Regime France. First, and most obvious, the king ruled as a divine monarch, with the sanction of the Church. French kings were crowned in the cathedral at Reims and anointed with holy water, in ceremonious symbol of the king as the spiritual and political leader of the kingdom. The relationship between Church and State was a very strong one. The king appointed all archbishops, bishops, abbots and other high officials in the Church. The French Church (the Gallican Church) thus enjoyed a certain independence from the Vatican, an independence that the revolutionaries were to emphasize and strengthen.

The Catholic Church owned extensive property in Old Regime France, including farm lands (upon which it collected seigneurial dues), commercial property, industries, and urban real estate. Church properties constituted between 15 and 20 percent of all land in France, and these holdings produced an enormous income: "In good years the tithe alone netted the Church 130,000,000 *livres*, and its total income was about 300,000,000—equal to half that of the royal government" (Connelly, 44).

Religion and the Clergy

The clergy in France numbered approximately 150,000. It can be divided into two categories in two different ways. We can speak of the regular clergy (monks, friars, nuns) in contrast to the secular clergy (bishops, cardinals, parish priests); or we can distinguish the upper clergy (the 10,000 bishops, abbots, cardinals, etc.) from the lower clergy (again, the parish priests and vicars). The regular clergy was widely resented or scorned in the 18th century, partly due to the large landholdings that a number of monasteries and convents had acquired, and partly because many of these clergy seemed to have strayed from the vows of poverty, abstinence and chastity that had formerly guided their behavior.

The upper clergy, too, was resented, but perhaps as much by the lower clergy as by those outside the Church. In the 18th century the upper clergy was almost entirely noble (the Church was a preferred vocation for younger sons of the aristocracy who would not inherit the family estate) and lived very comfortably, sometimes lavishly. The parish priests, by contrast, lived according to the resources, and generosity, of their parish, and this often meant a life of poverty. The upper clergy was largely out of touch with the people of France, while the lower clergy was largely out of touch with the wealth of the Church. In 1789 the upper clergy almost universally opposed the Revolution, while many of the lower clergy rallied to the cause of the Third Estate.

IDEOLOGICAL ORIGINS OF THE FRENCH REVOLUTION

The ideological origins of the French Revolution are largely to be found in the 18th-century critique of the social, political, and religious institutions we have just described. That critique, and the body of abstract thought that accompanied it, is generally referred to as the Enlightenment, a label which itself requires some explication. The term "enlightenment" derives from the phrase by which the French describe this century: *le siècle des lumières,* or the "century of lights." This is not an altogether helpful description for English speakers, and American scholars have suggested other labels for the period, such as "Age of Reason." This label, too, is problematical. It suggests the deductive thinking of 17th-century rationalism, epitomized in the dictum of René Descartes, "I think therefore I am." Enlightenment thinkers, by contrast, championed inductive thinking, the notion that knowledge derives not from the human mind alone, but rather from experience, experiment, and observation. Immanuel Kant, the late 18th-century German philosopher, termed the Enlightenment a "daring to know," a phrase that captures nicely the spirit of the times. For a somewhat fuller description of what the Enlightenment thinkers represent, we might profitably consider the following words of Norman L. Torrey:

> The main tenets of the group were a firm belief in the idea of progress, the application of the experimental method in science, the free and unfettered use of the God-given faculty of reason in all affairs, human and divine, and the ardent faith that reason, with all its limitations, was the final judge and the best guide available for the conduct of life.
>
> (Torrey, 10)

Out of these convictions emerged a compelling indictment, from several quarters, of religious intolerance, monarchical despotism, and social inequality.

The Enlightenment did not, of course, materialize out of thin air, and at this point we should consider some of the intellectual forerunners of this movement. Of particular importance is a collection of breakthroughs in observation and theory in the 16th and 17th centuries that are generally referred to as the Scientific Revolution. Without attempting a thorough discussion of this revolution in thinking, we might mention some of the more important figures and their contribution. These would include the Polish scientist Copernicus, who proposed a theory of the universe in the 1540s (based upon observation) that placed the sun, rather than the earth, at the center of our solar system; Galileo, who developed a rudimentary telescope in the early 17th century, adding to our knowledge of the moon and planets, and who also placed observation of the physical world on a mathematical path, as in his observations with regard to gravity; and the English scientist, Isaac Newton, who formulated the mathematical laws of gravity, and more generally the laws of modern physics, in his pathbreaking book *Principia Mathematica* (1687). Newton, like Galileo, pictured the universe as a machine, a natural order governed by mathematical laws. This Newtonian vision prompted many Enlightenment thinkers, most prominently Voltaire, to embrace Deism, a religious belief that posited a "watchmaker" God who created the world, but then left it to run according to natural laws. These thinkers, and others like them, challenged the traditional, religious conception of the world (which included a God who intervened regularly in the affairs of humans), and their revolutionary ideas were greeted initially by skepticism and hostility. Galileo, for example, was tried for heresy by the court of the papal Inquisition, and the Copernican theory of the universe was not accepted by the Church until the 19th century.

Another important influence on Enlightenment thought was the English philosopher John Locke. In his *Essay Concerning Human Understanding* (1690) Locke argued that a person at birth was like a *tabula rasa*, a blank slate waiting to be written upon.

Human knowledge, and human character, were not innate, but rather the product of education and environment. Human nature was not inherently evil, as the Biblical doctrine of original sin suggested, but rather inherently good, or at least neutral. Locke also argued, as our own Declaration of Independence would later assert, that man possessed the natural and inalienable rights of life, liberty, the pursuit of happiness, and private property.

The Enlightenment itself was an 18th-century movement, dominated by Frenchmen but not exclusively French. Beyond France's borders we might note the Scotsman David Hume, the Germans Immanuel Kant and Gottfried Lessing, and the Americans Benjamin Franklin and Thomas Jefferson, both of whom made lengthy visits to France. The French Enlightenment thinkers, or *philosophes* as they were known ("men of letters" might be a good translation), were essentially social critics, not philosophers. Although they often wrote abstractly, they were nearly all concerned with the reform of French society. We will consider five of the more prominent of these French *philosophes*.

Francois-Marie Arouet (1694-1778), known to contemporaries and posterity as Voltaire, was the son of a rich Paris lawyer. His satirical wit and sharp tongue offended both his father and the Church censors, and early in his life he experienced both temporary exile (to Holland) and an eleven month stay in the Bastille. Although Voltaire spent much of his life in exile (in England, Prussia, and Geneva), he still managed to secure election to the *Académie Française* and served briefly as the court historian of Louis XV.

Voltaire wrote poetry, plays (some called him the greatest playwright of the century), novels, historical works, and critical essays. He is most noted for his consistent attack upon religious intolerance and dogmatism. In *Letters Concerning the English Nation* (1733) he applauded the religious tolerance of Pennsylvania Quakers. His most celebrated work, *Candide*, includes a lampoon of the Spanish Inquisition. In the 1760s he defended in print the Protestant Jean Calas, accused of murdering his son because of his wish to convert to Catholicism.

In the year of Calas' conviction and execution Voltaire published his *Treatise on Toleration* (1763). Although Voltaire failed to save Calas, he did win mercy for his family and eventually succeeded in having the verdict reversed.

Charles Louis de Secondat, Baron de Montesquieu (1689-1755), was born near Bordeaux into a noble family. He earned a law degree, lived and wrote in Paris for some years, and in 1713 returned to Bordeaux to accept his inheritance of the family estate and the position of President of the Parlement of Bordeaux. Montesquieu is best known for his critique of absolutism, first suggested in the *Persian Letters* (1721) and more fully developed in his famous work, *The Spirit of the Laws* (1748). The *Persian Letters* was a satire of the monarchy and French elite society at the end of the reign of Louis XIV. In order to avoid censorship Montesquieu published the work anonymously, and employed the literary device of two Persians visiting Paris and then writing letters about what they saw and heard. Their references to the despotic regimes of Turkey and Persia made the French king appear only slightly better.

Montesquieu devoted most of the next twenty-five years to the preparation of his masterpiece, *The Spirit of the Laws*. He read voraciously in Greek and Roman sources, and spent two years in England during his research for this project. The book is essentially a study of law and political science. Based upon his observations in England, Montesquieu advocated a government embodying balance and separation between the executive, legislative, and judicial branches. Virtue for Montesquieu meant justice, and justice required a written body of law. In France Montesquieu argued that the ancient constitution (a traditional constitution, not a written one) no longer restrained an increasingly despotic monarchy. He urged a return to constitutional monarchy, in particular stressing the importance of intermediary bodies between king and subjects. The group most able to advise and restrain the monarch would be the aristocracy (indeed it was their natural duty), and the bodies through which they might exercise that role would be the *parlements*. Montesquieu, we might remind ourselves, was both an aristocrat and president of the Bordeaux *parlement*.

Montesquieu's political influence is very clear. Catherine the Great acknowledged his influence on her efforts to recodify Russian law. The impact of his work is apparent in the American Constitution and Bill of Rights. And the French Declaration of the Rights of Man and the Citizen and the Constitution of 1791 also bear the imprint of Montesquieu's theory of government.

Jean le Rond d'Alembert (1717-1783) and Denis Diderot (1713-1784) were co-editors of the most important publication in France during the 18th century, the *Encyclopedia*. Diderot was born in Langres, just north of Dijon, the son of a master cutler. He was extraordinarily well educated—proficient in many languages; a student of mathematics, physics, chemistry, and biology (some of his writings foreshadowed Darwin); a novelist, playwright, and poet. The name d'Alembert suggests nobility, but in fact he was an illegitimate child, named for the church upon whose steps he was abandoned. D'Alembert was a genius in mathematics, and it was that talent for which Diderot invited him to assist in their great publishing venture.

The *Encyclopedia*, published from 1751 to 1772, numbered some twenty-eight volumes, seventeen of text and eleven of illustrations. Initially published openly, in 1759 it encountered the wrath of the censor and thereafter was published abroad and smuggled into France. Some of the articles were philosophical in tone (entries such as "political authority," "liberty," and "religion" for example), but many more were scientific or practical in nature (entries such as "metallurgy," "farmers," and "asparagus," for example). More than 160 writers contributed to the project, virtually all of the great names of the Enlightenment.

As Diderot put it, the purpose of the *Encyclopedia* was "to collect all the knowledge scattered over the face of the earth, to present its general outlines and structure to the men with whom we live, and to transmit this to those who will come after us..." (Gendzier, xi). By this effort to define all human knowledge, and to make public previously private information (such as the techniques of a master craftsman), Diderot and his collaborators implicitly challenged the prerogative of the absolute monarch and the inherently private nature of corporate society. This was an ambitious endeavor, but the editors also acknowledged their own limitations, indeed those of humankind generally. Diderot promised an outline of the structure of human knowledge, yet the *Encyclopedia* was organized alphabetically, a purely arbitrary device. One could not possibly know everything, but one could attempt to master that knowledge relevant to human experience, knowledge of some utility. This is what the encyclopedists set out to do. The idea of progress was also implicit in the *Encyclopedia*—we may not know everything today, it suggested, but human knowledge is expanding with each passing moment.

By the 1780s there were some 15,000 copies of the *Encyclopedia* in France. It was an expensive collection (not everyone could afford it), but anyone with intellectual pretensions would have had access to a copy in a library or reading society. By its willingness to challenge authority, to question dogma and tradition, to attack ignorance and intolerance, the *Encyclopedia* epitomized the essence of the Enlightenment and helped form the intellectual climate in which the French Revolution occurred.

No discussion of the French Enlightenment would be complete without mention of Jean Jacques Rousseau (1712-1778), although there is considerable disagreement over his place in the Enlightenment, given his personal antagonism with Voltaire and his unwillingness to accept the *philosophes'* faith in reason and human progress. Rousseau was born in the Swiss city of Geneva, the son of a watchmaker. Rousseau's mother died within days of Jean Jacques' birth, leaving him in the care of a father who instilled in his son a love of books, but did not provide him with a sound education. In 1722 a personal quarrel forced Rousseau's father into exile, and the ten-year-old boy went to live with an uncle. At the age of sixteen Rousseau, too, left his birthplace. Rousseau idealized Geneva in his later years and longed to return, but never succeeded in doing so. In a very real sense he remained throughout his life a man without a home.

In his early years Rousseau worked as an apprentice, a servant, a music teacher, and a tutor, but with no great success in any of those occupations. In the 1740s he journeyed to Paris, where he met and befriended Denis Diderot, who commissioned several articles on music from Rousseau for the *Encyclopedia*. Diderot also inspired Rousseau to enter the 1749 essay contest sponsored by the Dijon Academy. Rousseau's *Discourse on the Arts and Sciences* argued that "all progress in the arts and sciences had contributed to the moral corruption of man" (Torrey, 121). The essay won first prize.

Rousseau entered the Dijon contest again in 1755, with his *Discourse on the Origins of Inequality among Men*. In this essay Rousseau pursued the iconoclastic line of argument begun six years earlier, claiming that society had corrupted the natural goodness of man and deprived him of his freedom. Even in this pessimistic argument, however, one could find a ray of hope. Since man had created society—it was not a "natural" creation, as Plato and Aristotle had argued—man could also reform, or regenerate, society.

If the *Second Discourse* was a scathing indictment of 18th-century European society and government, the *Social Contract* (1762) offered an abstract formula for the creation of an ideal society. The false social contract, imposed by the strong upon the weak, could be replaced, Rousseau argued, by a true social contract that would replace natural liberty with moral, or civil, liberty, and replace natural inequality with moral, or civil, equality. This would be difficult to achieve—Rousseau was not optimistic about the prospects for it. Given the existing corrupt state of society, initially the good services of a "Legislator" might be required, someone who, like Lycurgus or John Calvin, could rise above that corruption to introduce a legitimate social contract. Thereafter the "general will" (not the rule of the majority, necessarily, but in a more abstract sense the voice of the people, thinking of the good of all) would ensure that government worked for the good of the nation and not for individual interests.

It is Rousseau's political writing that draws our attention today, and that has made him one of the most written about figures in world history. But during his lifetime his fame, and it was considerable, derived principally from his novels, *La*

Nouvelle Héloise (1761) and *Émile* (1762). In all of his works, though, the political and the fictional, Rousseau developed the same themes. Having been so dependent himself in his early life—on patrons, masters, and mistresses—Rousseau insisted that the greatest ill for any man was to be dependent on someone else. In the natural state man did not need anyone, he was completely self-reliant. This could obviously never be true in society, but through the general will, and the creation of a code of laws, man could in a sense be dependent on a thing—the law—and on all people rather than one person. The law would itself be dependent on nobody because it would be dependent on everybody. Rousseau also wrote of the need for a revival of public virtue and social responsibility. As James Miller has suggested in the subtitle of his book, Rousseau was a "dreamer of democracy," not convinced, perhaps, that democracy could work in a country as large as France, but also not convinced, like most political thinkers of his day, that democracy must inevitably lead to mob rule, or anarchy, as it had in Athens at the end of the Peloponnesian War. Miller's title also suggests the romantic side of Rousseau, who believed that emotions and passions were as important a part of human character as reason.

What was the relationship between these Enlightenment thinkers and the French Revolution? First we must emphasize that the Enlightenment did not *cause* the Revolution. The *philosophes* were reformers, not revolutionaries. Despite their critique of the French monarchy, virtually all of them, with the possible exception of Rousseau, were profoundly skeptical of the people's ability to govern themselves. Their ideal government would be enlightened monarchy or an aristocratic republic. Although they attacked the Catholic Church as an institution, the *philosophes* generally viewed religion as essential to the preservation of public morality and social order. Far from being levelers, the *philosophes* viewed social hierarchy as natural.

While the *philosophes* and their ideas cannot be said to have caused the Revolution, certainly their writings influenced the revolutionaries as they struggled to create a new constitution and a new political order. Alexis de Tocqueville has argued that that influence was ultimately negative. In his view, the centralizing monarchy had grown so despotic by the 18th century that politics in France had virtually ceased to function, leaving a politically inexperienced population. The *philosophes*, writing in their libraries, were so out of touch with political reality that they advocated political and social reforms so hopelessly idealistic that the revolutionaries, in their struggle to attain those ideals, were doomed to failure (Tocqueville, Part Three, Chapter 1).

This view has been challenged from several directions. Some have argued that the influence of the *philosophes* was simply much less than has generally been assumed, and that their abstract idealism thus explains little about the Revolution itself (e.g., MacDonald). Others have argued that there was an underside to the Enlightenment, a "Grub Street" press with a much wider readership than the *philosophes* enjoyed and that this literature, too, had an impact on revolutionary politics (e.g., Darnton). Finally, a large body of recent scholarship suggests that politics had not ceased to function in the last decades of the Old Regime. On the one hand one sees a revival of the *parlements*, particularly the *parlement* of Paris, as restraints upon royal authority. First in the 1750s, over an issue of religious intolerance, and then in the 1770s, when Chancellor Maupeou attempted to squash the independence of the *parlements*, these judicial courts mounted an open and forceful challenge to monarchical despotism, and developed in their remonstrances to the king a theory of constitutional monarchy. On the other hand one sees that in this same period royal ministers and the *parlements* increasingly appealed to public opinion in support of their policies. It is difficult to define just who the public was, or how it might assert its political influence, but even the monarchy seemed to acknowledge its legitimate role, an acknowledgement that implicitly called into question the absolute authority of the king. One also sees in the 1780s the emergence of a more active periodical press—including pamphlets and newspapers—that foreshadowed the revolutionary press of the 1790s. Clearly all of these trends must be counted among the ideological origins of the French Revolution.

CAUSES OF THE FRENCH REVOLUTION

Why did the French Revolution happen? We come at last to our first major question. The answer, on the most general level, is that Old Regime government just quit working. There are reasons why this happened, though, and they involve cultural, social, economic, and political factors. These can be divided into long-term structural causes, and short-term circumstantial causes. Naturally these overlap—we don't want things to be too neat!

Many of the structural causes relate to the economic expansion and social change of the 18th century, which also help to explain why the Enlightenment writers found such a receptive audience in France. The years between 1725 and 1775 were growth years for France. Agricultural productivity rose 25 to 50 percent; commercial trade increased astronomically, by approximately 400 percent; industrial production also increased modestly, led by textile production, up 50 to 75 percent. Demographic growth accompanied this economic expansion—population grew by about 30 percent over the course of the century. Economic prosperity accounts for some of this population growth, but we should also note the disappearance of the plague from France after 1720, the absence of a major famine after 1709, and the fact that the century was relatively peaceful, particularly in comparison to the war-torn decades that ended the reign of Louis XIV.

The impact of this economic and demographic expansion was not entirely favorable. The economic growth had been fueled in part by the import of silver from the New World, and this produced inflation, a phenomenon that we may take for granted in the 20th century, but one that people of the 18th century viewed with great alarm. Between 1726 and 1789 land rents rose 82 to 98 percent, varying from province to province, while agricultural prices rose only 60 percent. Leases tended to be long-term in this period, which meant that landlords suffered while prices rose and the rents remained fixed, and then recouped their losses with a dramatic rent increase at the end of the lease, which occasionally forced tenants off the land, into the ranks of day laborers. The century witnessed a modest decline in the number of small holdings in France, though nothing so dramatic as the consolidation of landholdings that the enclosure movement produced in England. The cost of living generally rose 62 percent during this period, while wages rose only 25 percent. Both urban workers (a relatively small proportion of the population) and tenant farmers, then, suffered during this inflationary period.

Those who benefited most from this expansion were landowners, at least overall, and the urban bourgeoisie, which itself expanded during the century. The merchant class, obviously, flourished in the big cities. Urban areas grew more than rural areas, largely due to migration from countryside to town. On the eve of the Revolution there were 30 towns in France with a population exceeding 20,000 (see Map 3). These towns had become dynamic cultural and intellectual centers. Versailles no longer dominated the social and cultural life of France as it had in the 17th century. That honor had fallen to Paris, and even provincial towns had become more vibrant.

Urban growth contributed to a rise in literacy over the course of the century. Female literacy rose from 14 percent to 27 percent, male literacy rose from 29 percent to 49 percent, and overall literacy rose from 21 percent to 37 percent. There were 21 universities in France in 1789, secondary schooling was widely available, and virtually every major town boasted its own learned academy, where the educated elite could gather to discuss the latest books and their own research. Without this increased reading public, the ideas of the Enlightenment and the political debates between the *parlements* and the monarchy would have had a much diminished impact.

MAP 3: Thirty Largest Towns in France

The monarchy itself was plagued by certain structural problems that contributed to the revolutionary crisis. As noted above, Louis XIV had ruled without a prime minister, preferring to fill that role himself. Under Louis XV and Louis XVI that arrangement had led to ministerial infighting, with ministers vying for influence with the king and not infrequently undermining each others' policies in the process. The lack of ministerial cooperation proved catastrophic during the financial crisis of the 1780s. Another problem was the increasing insularity of the monarchy, both because Louis XVI tended to select his ministers from within court circles, and because the king disliked travel. Versailles, built as a symbol and showcase for the monarchy, had become in a sense a prison. Louis XV rarely left the palace, and when he ventured to one of the other royal chateaux he always avoided entering Paris; and Louis XVI left the Versailles/Paris region only once—a 1785 trip to Cherbourg, in Normandy. How could a king who refused to travel effectively govern a kingdom as diverse as France? Finally we should note the element of personal character that renders all inherited monarchies vulnerable. Louis XIV was an extraordinary leader, possessed of great energy and talent. Louis XV took little interest in governing, and Louis XVI, though more conscientious about affairs of state, was not a very capable ruler.

A final structural problem, suggested above, lay in the inefficient system of taxation. Certainly it was not a rational system but rather a hodgepodge of direct and indirect taxes, and the widespread perception was that the nobility and clergy did not pay their fair share. The tax farming system meant that the royal treasury never received a large portion of the taxes actually collected. In addition, France had no central bank, so that in times of revenue shortfall the monarchy borrowed money on less than favorable terms. Finally, the royal treasury had no official budget—no one really knew how much the government was collecting or spending. This entire system made it very difficult to respond effectively to the financial crisis that hit in 1786.

This brings us to the short-term causes of the French Revolution, for it is precisely in the financial arena where long-term and short-term causes most clearly overlapped. In the late 1770s the French monarchy sent both financial and material aid to the American colonies in their struggle for independence from the British crown. This was an opportunity for France to help weaken its chief rival, England, and to avenge in some small measure the loss of its own colonies in the Seven Years' War (the French and Indian War in North America). Louis XVI's finance minister, Jacques Necker, financed this aid by levying a second *vingtième* tax in 1776, and by contracting a number of short-term loans, scheduled to fall due in the late 1780s and 1790s.

When Necker resigned his post in 1781 he published an accounting of the royal budget, which showed a modest surplus in the treasury. Either Necker misread the situation (a definite possibility, given the lack of a unified accounting system) or he misrepresented it intentionally, for just five years later it became clear to a new finance minister, Charles Alexandre de Calonne, that the royal treasury was in serious trouble. He estimated 1786 revenue at 475 million *livres*, a deficit of nearly 25 percent. For 1787 Calonne projected that interest on the debt would absorb 50 percent of taxes collected, and that 50 percent of the anticipated tax revenue had already been spent in advance.

Further borrowing was obviously no solution to this problem, nor, for complicated reasons, could the king simply repudiate the debt, a measure to which kings had resorted in the past. Raising taxes was also not an option, first because the *vingtième* had already been increased three times; and second because France was not at war, the customary justification for a tax increase. When word began to circulate that the king and his ministers proposed to tax the Church and the nobility, the *parlement* of Paris announced that it would oppose such an action. Faced with this impossible situation, Calonne blamed Necker for mismanagement while Necker accused Calonne of incompetence and defended his own record—a classic instance of royal ministers appealing to public opinion for support. Public opinion could not, however, solve the problem, and so Calonne persuaded the king to convoke an Assembly of Notables in February 1787.

The Assembly of Notables was a carefully selected group of 144 men, including 7 princes of the blood, 14 bishops, 36 titled noblemen, 12 intendants and councillors of state, 38 magistrates from the *parlements*, 12 representatives from *pays d'état*, and 25 mayors. Calonne presented to this distinguished group an ambitious program, calling for tax reform, the abolition of internal tariffs, and creation of provincial assemblies. Louis XVI and Calonne expected willing approval from the Notables, but did not get it. Led by Loménie de Brienne, the Archbishop of Toulouse, the Notables countered with their own proposals and ultimately insisted that they lacked the authority to enact tax reform. Frustrated by this obstruction, Louis dismissed Calonne, who had already fled to London, and replaced him with Brienne, who surprised everyone by adopting virtually all of Calonne's program and attempting to force it through. Brienne, too, failed and in May 1787 dissolved the Assembly of Notables. The monarchy's serious effort to reform governmental structures had collapsed. The public now joined the Notables in calling for a meeting of the Estates-General, representatives of each of the three estates from throughout the kingdom, traditionally convoked by royal command in order to advise the king.

The fiscal crisis was not the only problem confronting the monarchy in 1787. The economy had been in a slump since 1775 and the situation was growing critical. The proposal to eliminate internal tariffs was one royal response to that problem. A second was a trade treaty with England, signed in 1786. Since 1775 France had been experiencing a wine glut, making it difficult for winegrowers to sell all their product and forcing prices down. The 1786 treaty called for England to lower tariffs on French wine and for France to do the same on British textiles. French winegrowers may have benefitted by this treaty, but the French textile industry undeniably suffered. British textile production was much more advanced than the French at this time, and British cloth undersold French goods even in French markets. The treaty went into effect in 1787 and within a year had produced massive unemployment in the textile towns of northern France—towns like Rouen, Troyes, and Elbeuf—adding to the general discontent.

As if these problems were not enough, disaster befell the agricultural sector as well. 1788 brought the worst harvest since 1709. Only the year before Brienne had acceded to a part of the Physiocrats' program by introducing free trade in grain. This untimely reform caused dramatic price increases in 1788, and rumors spread among the peasantry of a cruel conspiracy to starve them to death. In the Limousin a harsh freeze killed many chestnut trees, eliminating the traditional sustenance of those too poor to afford grain. Grain prices rose relentlessly, reaching their peak in July 1789.

A huge national debt, urban unemployment, crop failure and famine—all of these, combined with the structural weaknesses and contradictions of the monarchy, forced Louis XVI to convoke the Estates-General for the spring of 1789, a step that made revolution all but inevitable.

PART II:

THE FRENCH REVOLUTION

1789

This simple date—1789—has itself become a powerful symbol over the years. It has come to represent for many the Revolution as a whole, although the mood of 1789 was far different from the mood of 1793 or that of 1799. French revolutionaries in the 19th century distinguished sharply between 1789—the bourgeois revolution, an attempt to create a moderate, constitutional monarchy—and 1793—the people's revolution, a short-lived experiment in popular democracy that expired with the execution of Robespierre in 1794. The Revolution is in fact a complicated affair. It means different things to different people, then and now. For us 1789 represents the beginning of the Revolution, a momentous year that mobilized an entire nation.

Before dealing with 1789, however, we must return briefly to the last months of 1788. On August 8, 1788 Louis XVI issued his proclamation calling for a meeting of the Estates-General. Three weeks later the king recalled Jacques Necker as finance minister. The public looked favorably upon both decisions. Yet two important questions immediately confronted the public and the monarchy. How would the Estates-General be elected, and how would the deputies deliberate and vote once elected? No living person could readily answer those questions—the Estates-General had not met since 1614.

Louis XVI appealed to legal experts and archivists for answers to those questions, particularly with regard to the number of delegates that each of the three orders (Clergy, Nobility, and Third Estate) should elect. This was a thorny issue. Traditionally the three orders each sent the same number of delegates to the Estates-General, and voted in the assembly by order, not by head. There were now other precedents, however.

The provincial estates of Dauphiné had met that summer, with the Third Estate sending twice the number of delegates of the other two orders and the delegates voting by head, not by order. Some (exemplified by Rabaut Saint-Etienne's pamphlet that included the celebrated line, "history is not our code") argued that historical precedent was irrelevant, that the Estates-General should be convoked according to what was fair and just. The members of the *parlement* of Paris, who collectively were viewed as heroes by the public for their refusal to register new royal taxes, chose to ignore both Dauphiné and Rabaut Saint-Etienne. On September 25, 1788 it destroyed its popularity at a single stroke by ruling that the Estates-General should meet and deliberate exactly as in 1614. The *parlementaires*, theretofore viewed as champions of the people, now appeared to many as champions of narrow aristocratic ambitions, bent upon denying the legitimate aspirations of the Third Estate in order to reassert their own political power. Necker urged Louis to overrule the *parlement*, and in November he did so, calling for a "doubling of the Third," but saying nothing about the method of voting.

Throughout these months Paris was in an uproar, as people publicly debated the various issues and published pamphlets in support of their positions. Among the most influential of these was the pamphlet entitled "What is the Third Estate?," published by the Abbé Sieyés in January 1789. In it he answered the rhetorical question that the title suggested with a single word: "Everything," implying thereby that the aristocracy was nothing. In the following months observers increasingly viewed the approaching convocation of the Estates-General as a confrontation between the aristocracy and the Third Estate, led by the bourgeoisie.

On May 5, 1789 the Estates-General met at Versailles. Approximately 1200 delegates, half from the Third Estate, filed ceremoniously past the king to their seats in the meeting hall, the clergy and nobility dressed in their finery and the delegates of the Third Estate dressed drably in black. The delegates brought with them the *cahiers de doléances*, or grievance lists, that voters had drawn up in electoral assemblies throughout France at the request of the king. The nature of the elections—multi-stage, indirect elections in the case of the Third Estate—meant that the *cahiers* were relatively moderate, but they reflected consensus on a number of issues. They called for equitable taxation, judicial reform and reform of the seigneurial system. The *cahiers* of the clergy and nobility, while frequently expressing a willingness to pay their share of taxes, also asserted the legitimacy of traditional privilege. The *cahiers* of the Third Estate frequently mentioned specific fiscal or judicial grievances, but one would look in vain for any sort of revolutionary program in these *cahiers*. The most significant thing about the *cahiers* is that they had in a sense politicized the country—for several weeks people had given serious consideration to the problems confronting the country and had offered advice to the king. Now they expected Louis XVI to take their advice seriously.

Louis XVI received the *cahiers*, greeted the delegates, and ordered the three estates to reassemble in their separate meeting halls for the verification of credentials. Neither the king nor his ministers offered a program for reform. No strong leadership was evident, no clear direction was marked out. Nothing was said about the method of voting, but the separate meeting halls certainly suggested that voting would be by order, not head.

Alarmed at that suggestion, and disturbed by the lackluster opening of the assembly, the delegates of the Third Estate refused to verify credentials until the issue of voting was resolved. Six weeks passed with no apparent progress. Delegates sent pessimistic reports home to their constituents, and the mood grew increasingly restive. Led by the fiery orator, Honoré-Gabriel de Mirabeau, and the clever politician, Emmanuel-Joseph Sieyés, the Third Estate called for a written constitution, and on June 10 invited the other two estates to meet together with it. A number of parish priests, resentful of the power and affluent lifestyle of the upper clergy, rallied to the Third Estate. On June 17, heartened by that support, the Third Estate adopted the program set out six months earlier in Sieyés' pamphlet, and declared itself the National Assembly.

For three days the king did not respond, but on June 20 the Third Estate and their allies, including some liberal nobles, found the doors to their meeting hall locked, ostensibly so that preparations might be made for a royal session. Undaunted by this apparent royal challenge, the delegates gathered at an indoor tennis court, where they swore the famous Tennis Court Oath. Wherever they met there was the nation, they declared, and they would not adjourn until France had been given a new constitution. The first revolutionary steps had been taken. No longer an Estates-General, convoked by the king to give him advice, the delegates now called themselves deputies, members of a National Assembly intent upon creating a constitutional monarchy. The death knell of absolute monarchy in France had been sounded. In the royal session of June 23 Louis XVI seemingly accepted that agenda by calling upon the three estates to meet as one.

The deputies at Versailles could not hope to achieve their revolutionary agenda alone, however. Most of the bishops, and a large segment of the nobility, remained opposed to the program of the Third Estate. In the king's close circle two parties took shape. Necker and his supporters urged the king to compromise, allowing vote by head on issues affecting the nation as a whole. The queen and her party counseled Louis to hold fast to tradition and defend royal authority. Even in the June 23 decree the victory of the queen's party was apparent.

In the weeks that followed Louis ordered troops transferred from the frontiers to the vicinity of Paris, in order to control, or subdue, the unruly capital city. By the second week of July they numbered 20,000. On July 11 the king dismissed Necker, the favorite of the people, and ordered him out of the country (Necker was Swiss, but so were many of the royal troops). This news reached Paris the following day, and combined with the obvious troop movements convinced Parisians that a plot was afoot to dissolve the National Assembly. Camille Desmoulins, a radical idealist, called the people to arms, and the electoral assemblies that had met that spring went into action. Within a day a citizens' militia had formed and angry crowds roamed the streets, destroying the customs posts of Paris.

On the morning of July 14 a crowd of 80,000 moved first to the Invalides (the military hospital), where they seized arms, and then to the Bastille, the old royal prison that loomed over the lower-class neighborhoods of eastern Paris. The Bastille was virtually impregnable, its 100-foot walls surrounded by a wide moat. The crowd marched there not in the hope of freeing prisoners—there were only seven—but rather with the aim of securing ammunition. A portion of the crowd gained easy access to the outer courtyard, still outside the main walls and moat, and the governor of the Bastille, Count de Launay, received a delegation from city hall for lunch. De Launay agreed to withdraw his cannon from the prison walls, but refused to turn over the prison or its arms to the city. Meanwhile the crowd outside, uncertain of the fate of its emissaries, gained access to the inner courtyard. Royal troops now opened fire, killing ninety-eight people and wounding over seventy. De Launay, completely unprepared for such a crisis, at first took no action and then lowered the inner drawbridge and surrendered, in the hope that this would restore order. In the aftermath six soldiers were killed. De Launay received a safe escort to city hall, but there the crowd set upon him and killed him. They cut off his head, as well as that of Flesselles (a city official who had earlier denied arms to the crowd), and carried them about town on the end of pikes, a macabre lesson to those who would oppose the people.

The fall of the Bastille was more important for its symbolism than for the event itself. The people had not really conquered the fortress, it had fallen through the ineptitude of de Launay. The event sent shock waves through the court at Versailles, however. Royal troops in Paris had faltered in the face of the popular uprising, and the king now abandoned his intention to oppose the Third Estate by force. On July 15 Louis recalled Necker and withdrew the troops from Paris. Paris, more accurately the people of Paris, secured the victory first scored by the Third estate delegates at Versailles when they declared a National Assembly. Today July 14—Bastille Day—is celebrated as the French national holiday.

News of the fall of the Bastille spread quickly to the provinces, where rising grain prices and earlier reports of stalemate at Versailles had already caused alarm and social tensions. In some towns events came to a head before July 14, but in many it was the news of the Bastille that brought uprisings, the election of patriotic committees, and the formation of local militias (the future National Guards). These "municipal revolutions" meant that the king could not isolate Paris in the hope of undoing events at Versailles.

In the countryside, too, tensions mounted and emotions reached the breaking point. We should remind ourselves first of the economic crisis. The slump in the textile industry sent greater than usual numbers of unemployed workers, beggars, and vagrants wandering from village to town in search of alms or an odd job. The last month before the grain harvest (which came in late August) was always a difficult period, as families tried to stretch reserves until the grain had ripened. 1789, of course, was a particularly difficult year due to the previous year's poor harvest. The intrigues at Versailles and the armed uprising in Paris now cast those economic problems in a political light. Rumors spread through the countryside like wildfire that the aristocracy, determined at all costs to defeat the popular movement, had paid thieves and brigands to go into the fields and destroy the grain still green on the stalk, thus condemning the peasantry to starvation. This nefarious plot—the creation of desperate imagination—spread what Georges Lefebvre has called the "Great Fear" throughout most of France. The wandering beggars now appeared as brigands, and the panic added urgency to the campaign to form local militias. Peasants in many provinces seized upon this provocation to raid the châteaux of seigneurial landlords, where they typically destroyed the titles and deeds that documented the dues and services they so greatly resented. Often the peasants concluded their business with a stop in the lord's wine cellar. The Great Fear flared out almost as quickly as it began, lasting barely three weeks, but the violence in the countryside (directed mostly against property, not persons) made a strong impression on the deputies at Versailles.

A number of patriot deputies, alarmed by the reports of violence in the countryside, and convinced that the revolts might throw the nation into anarchy, made plans to grant to the peasantry the reforms that they demanded. Some hundred deputies were in on the secret plan, which called for action at an evening session on August 4. Two liberal nobles, the duc d'Aiguillon and the vicomte de Noailles (brother-in-law of Lafayette), addressed the Assembly in succession. They acknowledged the legitimate grievances of the peasants and, as large landowners themselves, generously pledged to relinquish their seigneurial privileges. In the wave of enthusiasm that swept over the hall deputies proposed the abolition of judicial privilege, of aristocratic hunting rights, of the tithe, and finally of all provincial and town privileges. The session came to an emotional close at two in the morning. The remnants of serfdom, seigneurial dues, tax privileges all had been eliminated in principle. As the decree issued on August 11 began, "The National Assembly destroys the feudal regime *entirely*." This was a bit misleading—serfdom survived in only a few provinces in 1789, and the feudal system had long ago ceased to exist formally, but this made the vestiges of feudalism all the more aggravating. In addition, seigneurial obligations were to be eliminated only after a redemption payment, though this requirement was ultimately dropped in 1793. Still, the night of August 4 was a momentous occasion, a victory for the peasantry and the symbolic end to the Old Regime system of privilege.

The National Assembly now turned its attention to the drafting of a statement of general principles upon which the new regime would be established. Mirabeau, Sieyés, and Lafayette each played a prominent role in the three-week discussion and debate that culminated, on August 26, in the Declaration of the Rights of Man and the Citizen. This document is the equivalent of the American Declaration of Independence. Criticized by opponents as being excessively abstract and general, it can in fact be read, as Georges Lefebvre has observed, as a rather pointed indictment of Old Regime society:

> [I]ndividual liberty is the subject of three articles, because administrative arrest and abuses of criminal procedure were a

menace to all. The rule of law was insisted upon because under the Old Regime there was no legal requirement which might not be somehow evaded at the king's discretion. Equality of rights was treated at length because special privilege was the foundation of the social hierarchy. The thought in the Declaration looked to the past more than the future.

(Lefebvre, 175)

The seventeen articles of the 1789 Declaration were expanded somewhat in later versions, and the tone of the document shifted with the tone of the Revolution itself (in 1793 the right to resist oppression was included as an inalienable right), but the Declaration of the Rights of Man and the Citizen still stands today as the symbolic foundation of the French Republic.

Louis XVI, prepared to take the offensive back in July, now found himself very much on the defensive in the face of these dramatic initiatives by the National Assembly. The king strongly opposed the decrees of August 11. As he put it, "I will not sanction decrees that would despoil my clergy or my nobility." He could be no more comfortable with the Declaration of the Rights of Man and the Citizen, the preamble to which made no acknowledgement of the authority of the monarch. Yet most of the deputies in the National Assembly assumed that these important documents required the signature of the king before they could be considered official. Louis simply refused to sign, and by doing so stalled the Revolution once again.

This stalemate produced the first divisions within what had come to be called the "patriot party." To date the Revolution had been propelled forward by armed uprisings, both in Paris and the provinces. But many deputies were clearly uncomfortable with the idea that legislators should appeal to the crowd in the streets at every difficult juncture. Yet without that recourse, how was the National Assembly to secure the approval of its legislation? Clearly the relationship between king and National Assembly needed to be resolved. Inspired by Montesquieu's advocacy of a separation of powers, moderates now proposed a two-chamber legislature, the upper chamber to be modeled on the aristocratic House of Lords in England. The king, they argued, should have an absolute veto. Radical deputies, inspired perhaps by Rousseau's notion of the general will and its inherent ideal of unanimity, favored a single-chamber legislature that would prevent the aristocracy from obstructing or dominating legislative action. Hopeful of gaining the support of Louis XVI, they proposed a suspensive veto for the king. The Assembly would be able to override the king's veto only by majority votes in three successive sessions.

The division within the National Assembly simply strengthened the king's resolve to procrastinate, and the legislative stalemate was ultimately broken by another intervention of the Paris crowd. The events of July had triggered the publication of a whole host of newspapers, and by late September several of the Paris papers had suggested that the king be brought to Paris, where the will of the people would be clearer to him. On October 5 the women of Paris took action on that suggestion.

Two days earlier, a Saturday, word had reached Paris of an October 1 banquet at Versailles hosted by the officers of the royal bodyguard. With the royal family in attendance, soldiers had reportedly thrown the revolutionary tri-color cockade on the ground, and replaced it on their hats either with a black cockade (the color of Austria, Marie Antoinette's homeland) or a white cockade (symbol of the Bourbon monarchy). This insult to the National Assembly aroused the anger of Parisian patriots, and when common women found bread in short supply at the Monday morning market, they decided to march the fifteen miles to Versailles. In short order some six to seven thousand women set out on the road from Paris.

By noon the alarm had been sounded throughout the city and a crowd soon gathered at city hall. Lafayette, now commander of the Paris National Guard, resisted the cries for an armed march to Versailles, but hotter heads prevailed and at five o'clock he set out on the path of the women at the head of 20,000 guardsmen. The women, of course, had by then arrived at Versailles, where they discovered that the king was off hunting. Upon his return Louis met with a delegation and assured them that Paris would be adequately provisioned with bread. Pleased at this response, and no doubt overawed by their audience with the king, the delegates failed to raise the issue of the king's return to Paris or his acceptance of the August decrees, much to the consternation of their companions outside.

At nine o'clock news reached the king of the approaching National Guardsmen. Some of the king's advisers counseled flight, an option that Louis seriously considered, but ultimately he viewed flight as an undignified action unworthy of his position. Instead, he sent word to the National Assembly that he would accept the August decrees, still unaware of the Guard's intention to escort him back to Paris. When the Guardsmen informed him of that plan the king responded with silence, and the royal family, deputies, women and guardsmen retired for the night with no resolution of the issue.

It was the crowd, again, that forced the issue next morning. Rushing past the posted guards they invaded the palace itself, reaching the antechamber of the queen's bedroom. The Swiss guards repelled the crowd, killing several, while the royal family retreated to safer quarters. The Parisians, determined to withdraw the king from the influence of reactionary aristocrats, pressed their demands for a return to Paris. Lafayette urged the king to follow that course and Louis finally acceded. That afternoon a long procession made its way through the rain and mud to Paris: the royal family, escorted by Lafayette, the women of Paris, the 20,000 National Guards, and some hundred deputies of the National Assembly, with the rest to follow shortly. Louis XVI and his family now took up residence in the Tuileries Palace, unoccupied for a century, where they would remain until August 1792. In these October days Paris had reasserted its primacy in national politics. For the next five years neither the king, nor the national deputies, would be able to ignore the will of the Paris crowd.

We have seen in the course of five short months the entire Revolution foreshadowed. Change occurred at a dizzying pace in this period. Virtually all of the groups that would be active in the following decade made their entry onto the historical stage between May and October. The aristocracy, which had in a sense initiated the political crisis back in 1787, for the most part adopted the conservative posture that would characterize it throughout the Revolution. The bourgeoisie, joined by liberal nobles and clergy, led the campaign at Versailles for constitutional and social reform. The peasantry, rising up in July and August, lent support to that effort and in addition secured the abolition of the seigneurial system. The Paris crowd, joined by the populace of other towns and cities, gave strength to the rhetoric of the deputies at Versailles and forced the king to accept the National Assembly and the August decrees. Without that popular uprising, the deputies would have been stymied in their efforts at reform. In the coming years, however, those deputies would struggle with the problem of how to control the Paris crowd (the revolutionary *sans-culottes*, as they came to be called).

No one would have predicted in May 1789 that five months later a National Assembly would be meeting in Paris with the king in residence nearby. The early events of the Revolution were unexpected to virtually everyone and terrifying to many. Yet even more dramatic changes would come over the next five years. By 1793 the monarchy had collapsed and the revolutionaries declared a French republic. Thousands of nobles, and other *émigrés*, had fled France for safety in other countries. The Catholic church, indeed the Catholic religion, was under attack. France was at war with most of the major European powers. By the end of 1793 a policy of revolutionary terror was in place. We cannot follow these events and developments in detail in the pages that remain. Rather we will focus on the major periods of the Revolution and try to establish the major accomplishments, and tensions, of each period. By this method we may hope to reach an understanding of the rise of Napoleon and the legacy of the Revolution for modern times.

CONSTITUTIONAL MONARCHY, 1789-1792

With the king and his family safely in Paris, the Constituent Assembly (the new name for the Estates General) could turn to the problems still confronting France and to the task of implementing in law the ideals set forth in the Declaration of the Rights of Man and the Citizen. By the end of its three-year term the Constituent Assembly had restructured the administrative, judicial, and tax systems of France and presented the nation with its first written constitution, by which the powers of the king were substantially limited. Compared to 1789, the next two years were calm and peaceful, although the period closed with a surge of popular unrest as the legitimacy of the constitutional monarchy was called into question, both by the king and by the Paris crowd.

These were the years of Mirabeau and Lafayette, ironically two liberal nobles (a count and a marquis), who played leading roles in the early Revolution. Mirabeau was perhaps the greatest orator in the Constituent Assembly, and his words helped shape the legislation of those years. Lafayette, who had fought alongside George Washington in the American Revolution, assumed command of the Paris National Guard and in that position exerted great influence over political affairs. Certainly there were many others who helped make the Revolution, but these two stand as symbols of the constitutional monarchy, and their careers are illustrative of how the course of the Revolution tended to outrun the political views of individual figures. In 1789 both of these men were in the vanguard of the Revolution, heroes to the populace and advocates of radical change. Two years later both were chiefly concerned with stopping the

FIGURE 1: Revolutionary Assignat

Revolution. On the eve of his death in April 1791, Mirabeau was secretly counseling Louis XVI to flee Paris and reassert his authority. He died a hero, but soon was branded a counterrevolutionary. One year later Lafayette denounced the radical republicans and fled into exile, to spend the rest of the revolutionary decade in an Austrian prison.

But we are getting ahead of ourselves. At the end of 1789 the most serious problem confronting France remained the national deficit. How was the treasury to be made solvent once again? In late October Bishop Talleyrand proposed what to many seemed an obvious solution: confiscate the property of the Church. Churches and cathedrals would not be touched, but income producing real estate, including monasteries and convents (monastic orders were to be abolished), would become the property of the nation, to be sold at open auction in order to generate revenue. The state, then, would take over education and charity (formerly the domain of the Church), and the clergy would be salaried by the government. Conservative bishops naturally opposed this legislation, which they viewed as a threat to the independence of the Church. Despite that opposition, the Constituent Assembly adopted Talleyrand's proposals.

Just how would the sale of church property, however, eliminate the national debt? To accomplish this the assembly issued a paper currency, the *assignats*, in large denominations to the government's creditors (see Figure 1). The assembly's original intention was that the *assignats* would be used to purchase Church lands (now known as *biens nationaux*, or national properties) at auction. The government would then burn the *assignats*, its creditors would receive property, and the debt would be liquidated. The *assignats* were not to be circulated, but speculators soon began selling them, at discount, for hard currency and this forced the assembly to issue smaller denominations for use in everyday exchange. Unfortunately this plan did not work out so neatly in practice. Survey and verification of national properties took time, and this delayed the sales for several years. In the meantime the *assignats* helped trigger an inflationary spiral, so that by 1794 they were worth approximately one quarter of their face value. Not until late in the decade did the national debt disappear—through inflation, the simple repudiation of a portion of the debt, and war booty.

The confiscation of Church property did indeed require a reorganization of the Church. The idea of a separation of Church and State did not even occur to most deputies. Rather, most argued, the state must assume the task of regulating Church institutions. The Civil Constitution of the Clergy, passed by the Constituent Assembly in 1790 and fully enacted in 1791, reduced the number of bishops to 83, mandated the public election of bishops and priests, stipulated a salary scale for clergy, and, since clergy were now essentially civil servants, required an oath of loyalty to the nation, the law, and the king.

The Civil Constitution threw the Church into an uproar. Nearly all of the seated bishops denounced it and called upon their parish priests to refuse the oath of loyalty, in their eyes a secular oath that violated their allegiance to a higher, spiritual authority. Fifty percent of the parish priests did refuse the oath (see Map 4). They were replaced by election, but many people rejected the new priests, and for a time the non-swearing priests (called refractory clergy) were allowed to conduct church services. This policy led to public disorder, however, and eventually refractory priests were ordered to leave the country or face forced exile.

Louis XVI, a devout Catholic himself, initially refused to sign the legislation, hoping that the Pope would guide him on this issue. For months Pope Pius VI remained silent, finally issuing a papal condemnation one day after Louis had signed the Civil Constitution into law. This deeply distressed the king, and strengthened his resolve to resist the Revolution.

The Civil Constitution of the Clergy created a crisis of conscience not only for the clergy but for many ordinary citizens as well. For some it now seemed necessary to choose between the Revolution and the Church. Revolutionaries viewed the bishops as actively advocating counterrevolution, and in some areas refractory priests did indeed lend moral support to opponents of the new regime. Geographically one finds a

Constitutional Monarchy, 1789-1792

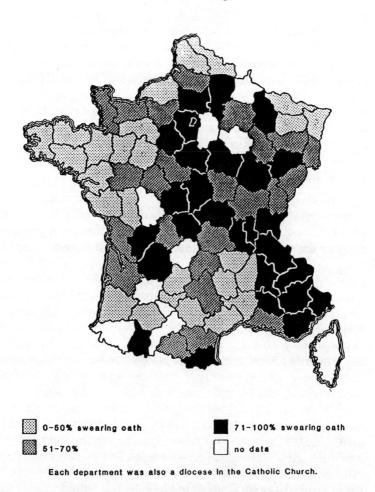

- 0-50% swearing oath
- 51-70%
- 71-100% swearing oath
- no data

Each department was also a diocese in the Catholic Church.

MAP 4: Revolutionary Departments and Response to Civil Constitution of the Clergy (1791)

substantial correlation between those areas where priests refused to swear the oath and areas of counterrevolution (as in the Vendée rebellion in western France or the Lozere in the south). The Church, unfortunately, had long been involved in matters of government and politics, and the resistance of bishops and clergy to the Civil Constitution provoked an attack upon Catholicism itself. By 1794 radical revolutionaries were pressing a de-Christianization campaign, closing down churches and cathedrals, or converting them to Temples of Reason. Not until Napoleon came to power did the French government finally make peace with the Catholic Church (in 1801-1802). Even so, the Concordat signed then could not erase the anti-clerical attitudes that the Revolution had awakened, and relations between Church and State remained troubled in France until early in the 20th century.

The Constituent Assembly also turned its attention to less controversial elements of reorganization. It replaced the old provinces by 83 departments (See Maps 2 and 4)—each of roughly the same size and named for distinguishing geographic features. This new set of boundaries was to be a rational administrative structure, as opposed to the traditional provincial boundaries that had no rhyme nor reason to them. It would also be a physical reminder that the Old Regime had disappeared, and that the new regime would be different. The citizens of each department would elect a departmental council, and within departments towns and districts also elected councils. A four-tiered system of representation thus came into being: national, departmental, district and municipal, and over the course of the Revolution one can follow the political careers of men as they moved from one level up to the next. The Constituent Assembly also created a new taxation system, ultimately to be administered by these local governments. Just as clergy and local officials were to be elected, so too were judges, and a new multi-tiered judicial system was put in place. Justice would now be the same for all, no longer determined by position or privilege. Consistent with the general attack upon privilege, the deputies also eliminated most government monopolies and tariffs, and abolished the guild system. Both of these measures tended toward the creation of a free, capitalist economy.

The principal task of the Constituent Assembly, of course, was to be the drafting of a constitution, and for two years the deputies labored at that task. The document presented to the nation in June 1791 was a moderate, liberal constitution. It called for the election of a Legislative Assembly, to be renewed every two years and to be composed of 745 deputies. The constitution distinguished between "active" and "passive" citizens. "Active" citizens—males over 25 who paid at least three days' wages in taxes—would be eligible to vote, although only those paying tax equivalent to ten days' wages could be elected. "Passive" citizens, while denied the vote, were equal before the law.

The king, the executive branch, was to be allowed only a three-year suspensive veto, which he could not apply to constitutional or fiscal legislation (hence his approval of the constitution was not required). He became in effect a civil servant, paid an annual salary of 8,000,000 *livres* by the state. The king had the power to declare war and appoint ministers, but only with legislative approval. The "absolute" powers of the king had dissolved in thin air, and for some, Louis XVI among them, the king as defined by the Constitution of 1791 was scarcely a monarch at all.

While guarding against despotism on the one hand, the Constituent Assembly seemed clearly concerned by the danger of popular democracy on the other. The right to vote, as already noted, was more restrictive than it had been in 1789. In addition, a revised Declaration of the Rights of Man and the Citizen accompanied the new constitution. Only the right to *peaceable* assembly was guaranteed; freedom of speech was similarly qualified; and the rights of the individual might be overridden by the needs of society.

Louis XVI was not impressed by these moderate tendencies in the Constitution of 1791. He felt like a captive in his own palace, distraught at the attack upon the Church, and dismayed at the loss of royal power. Urged by family, friends, and advisers to take action, the king made plans to flee Paris. Late on the night of June 20, 1791, Louis and his family disguised themselves as servants and left the Tuileries Palace by coach for the eastern border. Before they could reach the loyalist forces, hoping to restore the king to full power, Louis was recognized and apprehended at Varennes. The local National Guard held the royal family there until deputies arrived to escort the king back to Paris. The flight to Varennes (explained to the nation as an attempted kidnapping) prompted the Constituent Assembly to amend the constitution, adding clauses that would allow for a king's trial should he turn against the nation. Three months later Louis XVI swore a public oath to uphold the new constitution, and was paraded about the Tuileries garden on the shoulders of the crowd. But already at its formal inauguration the contitutional monarchy seemed destined to collapse.

On his flight in June Louis XVI had left behind a note denouncing not only the new constitution (which he subsequently swore to uphold!), but also the Jacobin Clubs, which he viewed as a threat to stable government. The first Jacobin Club formed in late 1789. Formally known as the Society of Friends of the Constitution, it derived its nickname from the Jacobin convents, in whose building the club met. By 1791 there were clubs in every major town in France, and by 1793 a network including hundreds of clubs would extend across the country. Largely composed of bourgeois men, they formed to discuss and debate public issues. Over time they became an effective lobbying force, an organized pressure group of sorts. Some argued that the Paris Jacobin Club acted like a shadow assembly, debating legislation before it came before the national assembly and influencing the deputies' votes. There is no doubt that the Paris club helped bring Maximilien Robespierre to national prominence in 1792-93. Another Paris club, the Cordeliers—boasting a less wealthy membership—served as home base for Robespierre's future rival Georges Jacques Danton.

The clubs were one of the key vehicles for the mobilization of popular politics in revolutionary France, but like most other public and political institutions of the era there was little place for women in them. Women under the Old Regime had been distinctly second-class citizens. Literacy among women was lower than among men, and those who did receive an education polished their social skills and studied the arts rather than the classics and sciences. Bourgeois and aristocratic women led lives of leisure, spent largely at home, and even peasant women, who worked as hard as the men, did most of their work in or near the household. Many young women found work as domestic servants, but only in the textile industry, and prostitution, did one find large numbers of women working away from the home. In most areas of France a woman's legal rights were assumed by her husband upon marriage. Some of the *philosophes* championed the cause of women. Montesquieu called for legal divorce, and Condorcet wrote an *Essay on the Admission of Women to Citizenship*. Rousseau, on the other hand, argued that the proper function of woman was to please man.

The Revolution did bring some changes in the status of women. The Jacobin clubs did not admit women as full members, but many did allow them to attend meetings. At least one club, the Society of Patriotic Women, was composed exclusively of women. Legislation passed in 1790 made it possible for women to inherit property, and the foundation was laid for equal education, although that goal was not even approached in France until late in the 19th century. These gains paled, however, against the reality that women were still not full citizens and could not vote. Indeed, the Declaration of the Rights of Man and the Citizen made no mention of women at all. This inspired Olympe de Gouges to publish, in September 1791, her Declaration of the Rights of Woman. The document, addressed to the queen, paralleled the articles of the original Declaration, modifying them somewhat and inserting "woman" in place of "man." The most stirring section of the document, however, is the postscript, in which de Gouges denounced the institution of marriage ("Marriage is the tomb of trust and love.") and pleaded the rights of illegitimate children. Perhaps this Declaration inspired the 1792 legalization of divorce, but it did not earn for de Gouges any lasting public honor. In 1794 she was executed as a royalist.

While the Revolution brought some gains for women—and one can arguably see the first signs of a conscious feminist position in this period—they virtually disappeared under Napoleon. The Napoleonic Civil Code established a legal double standard for women that endured in France until the 20th century. Napoleon is reported to have observed that "If there is one thing that is not French it is a woman who does what she wants." Napoleon, of course, was Corsican.

THE FALL OF THE MONARCHY

Louis XVI remained on the throne for more than a year after the flight to Varennes, but it was a troubled year. In July 1791 the Cordeliers club circulated a petition calling for the king's trial and a new government. On July 17 a large demonstration on the Champ de Mars got out of hand, and the National Guard, led by Lafayette, killed twenty people as it tried to restore order. This incident prompted Lafayette to resign from the Jacobin Club, grown too radical for him; at any rate, his popularity among Parisians was now in steady decline.

In September 1791 a new national assembly was elected, the Legislative Assembly. At Robespierre's suggestion, the Constituent Assembly had voted that none of its members would be eligible for reelection. Robespierre's goal was to exclude conservative royalists from the Legislative Assembly, and in this he largely succeeded. The new deputies were predominantly constitutional monarchists, and some leaned very soon toward republicanism. The leading faction within the Legislative Assembly, called Brissotins by some (after the deputy, Jacques-Pierre Brissot) and Girondins by others (after the department from which many of its leaders came—the Gironde, centered on Bordeaux) were wary of Louis XVI's intentions, but not yet convinced republicans.

One of the pressing concerns for the Legislative Assembly was the *émigrés*, aristocrats who had fled France early in the Revolution, some of whom were now gathered at the head of troops on the eastern borders. The king's flight to Varennes had apparently aimed at rallying those troops for a restoration of the absolute monarchy. The other monarchies of Europe also appeared ready to intervene on behalf of Louis XVI. This atmosphere helped to create a war party in Paris by late 1791.

The Girondins urged war as a way to test the king's loyalty to the new regime. Marie Antoinette urged war in the hope that defeat might bring the collapse of the Revolution and the restoration of her husband's full powers. On April 21, 1792 the king and Legislative Assembly declared war on Austria, the country that most aided the *émigré* nobles. Prussia soon joined in the war against France.

The war went badly for France. The officer corps had been decimated by emigration, and the rank-and-file soldiers were suspicious of those aristocratic officers who remained. Prussian and Austrian troops soon pushed the war onto French territory. Meanwhile, Louis refused to authorize measures against refractory clergy and *émigrés*, the apparent enemies of France. Convinced that the king was in secret collusion with the monarchs of Austria and Prussia, the clubs and section assemblies of Paris now called for an end to the monarchy. On June 20, 1792 the people of Paris mounted an assault on the Tuileries Palace. The uprising failed, and Lafayette rushed to Paris from the front to call for the abolition of the Jacobin Club. Instead the Legislative Assembly threatened him with trial for desertion, and Lafayette fled to Austria. The radical deputy Billaud-Varenne proposed on July 15 that the king be exiled, and a petition to that effect soon gathered the support of most of the Paris sections. Georges Danton now rallied the clubs and sections to action, and on August 10 a more organized assault was mounted against the Tuileries. Bolstered by volunteers from Marseille, the Paris crowd triumphed. Louis and his family sought the protection of the Legislative Assembly, which immediately called for new elections. The monarchy had fallen, and on September 21 the newly elected National Convention declared the first French Republic.

RADICAL REPUBLIC, 1792-1794

Even before the Convention could convene, Paris was racked by a wave of violence that soured the atmosphere in which the deputies would deliberate during the coming months. On September 2 news reached the capital of the fall of the fortress at Verdun. The path to Paris now appeared open to the Austrian and Prussian troops. Panic and fear gripped the population, and rumors spread that aristocrats and traitors in the prisons were plotting to attack patriot Paris from within. Taking justice into their own hands, the radicals of Paris invaded the prisons, conducted summary trials in the streets, and executed some 1,300 people, about half the prison population. This bloodletting shocked Paris and the provinces. Jean-Paul Marat, who had already offended moderates by the diatribes in his newspaper, now earned for himself the labels "anarchist" and "drinker of blood" for defending in print the September massacres. By the end of the month calm had returned to Paris, and victory at Valmy turned the tide against France's enemies on the battlefield. But the deputies in the National Convention would not forget the unrestrained violence that the Paris crowd had wreaked during those fateful September days.

The first task confronting the National Convention was the question of Louis XVI. What does one do with a former king? The deputies perceived three options. The Girondins argued that the king should be tried for his crimes against the nation. But the constitution of 1791 was ambiguous on this point, and conservative deputies insisted that Louis enjoyed royal immunity from trial. The radical Montagnards (Mountaineers), given that name because of their customary position high in the meeting hall, agreed with conservatives that the king should not be tried. They called for execution without trial, observing that Louis had already been tried in the streets of Paris. As the deputy Saint-Just put it, "No man can reign innocently." Many of the Montagnards were members of the Jacobin Club, and they were much more willing than the Girondins to turn to the Paris crowd for support.

The deputies voted to try Louis XVI, and after much debate decided that the National Convention would conduct the trial itself, rather than creating a special tribunal. A special commission was named to sift through royal papers in search of evidence and to prepare formal charges, a long process highlighted by the discovery in mid-November of a secret safe in the Tuileries Palace containing correspondence from the king and queen to other European monarchs. Louis XVI was charged with conspiracy against the nation. The trial lasted more than a month, from December 11, 1792 to January 15, and on two occasions the king spoke in his own defense. The deputies unanimously voted a verdict of guilty. The Girondins then proposed that the question of a sentence be referred to the nation by referendum, hoping in this way to spare Louis' life. The motion failed. How then should the king be punished—banishment, imprisonment, or execution? Strong arguments were put forward on all sides. The final roll call, on January 16-17, required over twenty-four hours, with deputies casting their votes, often accompanied by a short speech, one by one. By a vote of 387 to 334 the deputies sentenced the king to death. On January 21, 1793 Louis XVI ascended the stairs to the guillotine. He again proclaimed his innocence, pardoned his enemies, and went to his death with dignity. Marie Antoinette followed Louis to the scaffold in October.

The execution of the king allowed the National Convention to turn to its other principal task, the drafting of a new constitution. The trial of the king, however, introduced new complications and obstacles. Within a month of Louis' execution England, Holland, and Spain had joined Austria and Prussia in war against France, forcing the young republic to commit ever increasing resources, both material and human, to the war effort.

In addition the trial itself had deepened divisions within the National Convention. The Girondin faction was perceived by most people to have favored leniency for the king. Back in September Girondin deputies had denounced leading Montagnards, such as Robespierre and Danton, for their alleged involvement in the September massacres. Now, in a sense, the tables were turned, though the Montagnards did not hold a majority in the National Convention. The Montagnards did, however, enjoy much more support among the people of Paris and had a strong base in the Jacobin clubs as well. The Girondins were openly skeptical, if not scornful, of the political role of the Paris crowd. They were predominantly representatives of provincial departments. Between these two factions sat the moderate majority of the National Convention, deputies known collectively as the Plain, or more pejoratively, the Swamp.

Through the first five months of 1793 the Girondins controlled key positions within the Convention, but they were not strong enough to dominate. Factional disputes blocked legislative progress, and months dragged by without the adoption of a new constitution. The Girondins appeared to favor a federated structure of government with a restricted electorate, defined by property qualification. The Montagnards favored a strong central government and popular democracy, featuring universal male suffrage. Frustrated by this factionalism, departmental administrations sent letters and delegations to Paris imploring their deputies to end their differences and draft a new constitution.

The Girondins made the first move to break the stalemate by bringing impeachment proceedings against Jean-Paul Marat in April 1793. This move backfired. Marat was acquitted and the people of Paris, seeing their hero vindicated, took the offensive themselves. Petitions circulated in the clubs and section assemblies of Paris calling for the proscription of twenty-two deputies, nearly all Girondins. The Girondins countered by launching an investigation of this illegal conspiracy against national representatives, but the Paris crowd once again carried the day. Militant National Guardsmen and others surrounded the National Convention on May 31 and again on June 2, eventually forcing the deputies to proscribe twenty-nine of their colleagues, the leading Girondins. The Montagnards now controlled the National Convention—the people of Paris had pushed the Revolution another step to the left.

In this instance, however, the rest of France did not wholeheartedly follow the lead of Paris. In the west, the neighboring departments of the Vendée and Deux-Sèvres had been the scene of counterrevolutionary uprisings since March, when a military draft had been announced. Counterrevolution had also erupted in the south. Many departments now protested the proscription of the Girondin leaders, and in Caen, Bordeaux, Lyon, and Marseille (all located on the geographical periphery of France) "federalist" leaders called for an armed march on Paris. In most areas the "federalist" revolt fizzled out by late June, with the publication of a new constitution, but in Lyon and Marseille rebels held out until October, and repression of the revolt was harsh in both cities.

THE TERROR

Confronted by counterrevolution in the Vendée, "federalist" uprisings in several major cities, and a continuing foreign war on several fronts, the National Convention adopted emergency measures to defend the Revolution. Even before the "federalist" revolts the deputies voted to create two executive committees, known collectively as the Great Committees. The Committee of General Security, created in October 1792, was essentially a police committee. The Committee of Public Safety, the more powerful of the two, served as the executive branch of the government from April 1793 until August 1794. Georges Danton led the Committee of Public Safety between April and July 1793. He then resigned, however, and from July 1793 until July 1794 Maximilien Robespierre dominated the Committee, aided by his loyal supporter Saint-Just. Although the Committee was to be renewed at the end of each month, between August 1793 and July 1794 its membership did not change. This was the infamous Year II, the year of the Terror.

Early in September 1793, in the wake of another poor harvest and news from the southeast that royalists had turned the city of Toulon over to the British, the militants of Paris again rose up, demanding war on aristocrats and food hoarders. In response to that uprising, the National Convention made terror "the order of the day." One month later, at Saint-Just's initiative, the deputies voted that the government would remain revolutionary (i.e., the constitution would be suspended) until the end of the war. As it turned out this meant that the constitution of 1793, the most democratic of the Revolution, never went into effect.

Revolutionary government, government by terror, meant essentially two things. First, it meant price controls on staple goods and the creation of a revolutionary army to ensure an adequate supply of food to the cities. This was of particular importance to the people of Paris, who had seen their city dangerously under-supplied in the summer of 1793. Second, the Terror involved the suspension of many civil liberties, and the repression of those believed to be enemies of the Revolution. The Terror was not a "class" war aimed at former aristocrats (noble titles had been abolished in 1790), nor was it applied indiscriminately across the country. The Terror was most severe in areas of civil war, counterrevolution, and in some of the departments near the frontier. In some departments the Terror claimed fewer than ten victims. Seventy per cent of the death sentences were handed down in just five departments. In some areas the Terror was particularly harsh. In Nantes, near the center of the Vendée rebellion, Jean-Baptiste Carrier ordered the drowning of 2,000 suspected counterrevolutionaries. In Lyon over 2,000 were executed, some by guillotine and others shot down by cannon. Under the Law of Suspects, some 70,000 people were arrested during the Terror, roughly 0.5 percent of the population. Our best estimates suggest that 40,000 people were executed during the Terror.

We should also mention the two major political trials in Paris during the Terror. In March 1794 the Committee of Public Safety sent Jacques Hébert and his supporters before the Revolutionary Tribunal, where they were sentenced to death. Hébert, more radical than the Jacobin deputies, was a leader of the de-Christianization campaign that reached its peak in this period. He was a threat to the Committee of Public Safety from the left. In April Georges Danton went on trial, accused of corruption and conspiracy against the government. Danton had recently spoken out about the need to bring the Terror to an end. Radicals on the Committee—such as Billaud-Varenne and Collot d'Herbois—viewed Danton as dangerously moderate. Having executed Hébert, they argued, it was necessary to eliminate Danton in order to keep the Revolution on course. On April 5, 1794 Danton and 16 others went to their deaths. Less than four months later, as Danton predicted, Robespierre would follow him to the guillotine.

REVOLUTIONARY SYMBOLISM

For those living in France in the 1790s this whirlwind of change had to be extremely disorienting. The political, social, and cultural traditions of French society had been shattered. In the space of four years France had gone from absolute monarchy to constitutional monarchy to democratic republic to Jacobin dictatorship. The system of privilege and aristocratic titles had been abolished. Monarchical art—epitomized by Versailles—had given way to revolutionary art—epitomized, perhaps, by David's painting of Jean-Paul Marat, dead in his bath (Marat was assassinated by Charlotte Corday in July 1793, and thus became one of the martyrs of the Revolution).

In the midst of this rapid change, men and women tried to lend legitimacy to the new institutions, to create, as it were, a new tradition. They did this, in part, through the use of symbols. Unlike the American revolutionaries, the revolutionaries in France did not succeed in writing a constitution that would endure 200 years. The constitution of 1791 did not survive even two years, nor did the Declaration of the Rights of Man survive in its original form. These written documents did not create a new tradition for France. One might argue, indeed, that the French tradition over the next two centuries was a revolutionary tradition rather than a stable, constitutional tradition.

We must look, then, to other kinds of symbols, some of them official and some of them generated by the people themselves. Symbols were a way of focusing revolutionary enthusiasm and energy, of expressing revolutionary ideals and values. During the years of the Jacobin republic (1793-94) revolutionary symbols came into full flower, but they began to appear in the first months of the Revolution. The tricolor flag of France—red, white, and blue—has its origins in July 1789, when the colors of

Paris (red and blue) were joined to the white of the Bourbon monarchy. By 1793 it was mandatory to wear a tricolor cockade, a symbol of one's support for the Revolution. The planting of liberty trees also began in 1789, a symbolic act derived from the popular custom of erecting maypoles in spring as a fertility ritual. Liberty trees symbolized an end to the slavery of feudalism. The floppy, red Phrygian cap, given to freed slaves in Roman times, also became a symbol of revolutionary freedom. The very dress of the *sans-culottes*—long pants and wooden clogs instead of knickers and leather shoes—became an emblem of revolutionary loyalty by 1793.

As time went by a whole succession of revolutionary festivals came into being. July 14 (the fall of the Bastille), August 10 (the fall of the monarchy), January 21 (the execution of Louis XVI), and May 31 (the expulsion of the Girondin deputies) all became national holidays, commemorating the great events of the Revolution with parades, colorful floats, and colossal monuments. In July 1791, the second anniversary of the fall of the Bastille, Voltaire's body was transferred to Paris by chariot and laid to rest in the Pantheon. Busts of Rousseau could be seen in most of the Jacobin clubs. As new symbols appeared, old ones faded from view. After the flight to Varennes, statues of the French kings (most commonly Louis XIV) disappeared from public squares. And following August 10, 1792 *Place Royale* became *Place de la Liberte* in virtually every French town. In September 1793 the revolutionaries went so far as to change the calendar. September 21, 1792 became retroactively Day 1 of Year I, the founding of the Republic and of a new era. The new calendar reflected the reasoned thinking of the Enlightenment. The new months, with names like Brumaire and Floréal, corresponded to the changing seasons (see Chart 1).

All of these symbols and symbolic practices fulfilled a dual role. At the same time that they portrayed or reflected the new ideals and values of a revolutionary citizenry, they also represented to the people, particularly those not yet converted, just what the values of the new regime would be. Symbols, it was hoped, would lend legitimacy to that regime. It is particularly interesting that the new republic, born of violent revolution, should take as its central icon a feminine figure, Marianne, the symbol of revolutionary virtue.

Words, too, are symbols, of course, and never more so than during the Revolution. Liberty, equality, and fraternity became the bywords of the Revolution. "La Marseillaise," written in 1792 as a marching song to accompany the Marseille volunteers on their route to Paris, still survives as the French national anthem. Powerful orators could incite revolutionary crowds to action or sway votes in the National Assembly. Among the most powerful speeches of the Year II are those of Robespierre, particularly those that attempted to define public virtue and revolutionary government.

Year II	1793
1 Vendémiere	22 September
1 Brumaire	22 October
1 Frimaire	21 November
	1794
1 Nivôse	21 December
1 Pluviôse	20 January
1 Ventôse	19 February
1 Germinal	21 March
1 Floréal	20 April
1 Prairial	20 May
1 Messidor	19 June
1 Thermidor	19 July
1 Fructidor	18 August

CHART 1: Revolutionary Calendar

THE FALL OF ROBESPIERRE

Dramatic symbols and stirring rhetoric cannot, unfortunately, guarantee political stability. Very real political and social tensions endured in France, and were not resolved by the Jacobin government. By spring 1794 the regime had quelled counterrevolution at home and the revolutionary armies were carrying the war onto foreign territory. The nation appeared secure, yet the Terror continued and the constitution remained suspended. The Jacobin leaders, although they had ridden the shoulders of the Paris crowd to power, were concerned about the volatility of popular politics and anxious to bring the crowd under control. The trial and execution of Hebért, one of the heroes of the Paris crowd, was a part of that effort. The Terror, although called for by the people and carried out in the people's name, was used in part to control and suppress popular politics. The problem confronting Robespierre, and others on the Committee of Public Safety, was how to end the Terror. Even as the Terror eliminated enemies of the revolutionary regime, it created new ones. But as the case of Danton had shown, to oppose the Terror was to risk being branded a counterrevolutionary.

On July 26, 1794 Robespierre rose to the podium of the National Convention and announced that the Revolution was threatened once again, that conspirators were plotting against the government and must be exposed and punished. He named no names, but Robespierre's words were enough to bring together fearful deputies on the left and the right. The next day (9 Thermidor on the new calendar) Robespierre found himself accused before the Convention, and within twenty-four hours he, Saint-Just, and twenty-six others had gone to their deaths on the guillotine. The militants of Paris, either away at war or dismayed by Robespierre's recent policies, failed to rise in his defense.

Robespierre, rightly or wrongly, had come to symbolize the Terror, and with his death the Terror came to an end. Some would argue that the Revolution now came to an end as well. Five years remained, however, before Napoleon seized power, and we turn now to a brief consideration of those years, and the rise of Napoleon, as a conclusion to our text.

THE DIRECTORY REGIME AND THE RISE OF NAPOLEON

In the months following Robespierre's execution the National Convention drafted a third revolutionary constitution, which once again restricted the electorate to those who owned property. Property owners, it was argued, would be the best educated and most responsible citizens. The moderate deputies who now dominated the National Convention clearly feared the role of the crowd in politics. Equally conscious of the dangers of centralized government, the deputies instituted a clear separation of powers between executive, legislative, and judicial branches and created a five-man Directory to hold executive power. The new constitution stressed the duties of all citizens more than their rights, and made no mention of the right to insurrection against an oppressive government. It created a two house legislature—the Council of Elders, an upper house that would be composed of 250 men aged 40 or older; and the Council of 500, composed of members at least 30 years of age. Had these age requirements been in effect earlier in the Revolution, Saint-Just, among others, would not have been elected—he was only 27 at his execution. The Council of 500 was to initiate all legislation, the Council of Elders could only accept or reject proposed laws.

To guard against a royalist resurgence the National Convention mandated that at least 2/3 of the deputies in the new legislature be ex-members of the Convention. Some viewed this as rather self-serving, and it helped build support for a royalist uprising in Paris on October 5, 1795, just three weeks before elections. To put down the uprising the leaders of the Convention called upon Napoleon Bonaparte, who dispersed the crowds with his celebrated "whiff of grapeshot."

The regime of the Directory ruled France for four years. It is seldom given credit for the domestic reforms, educational programs, and foreign policy successes that are a part of its record. Historians have tended to emphasize the war profiteering, political corruption, and social decadence that characterized Paris society, relieved at seeing an end to the Terror and determined to celebrate. This was the era of victims' balls, open only to those who had lost a relative to the guillotine. Those in attendance wore black ribbons around their necks. This symbolic "counter Terror" was accompanied by a very real White Terror in the countryside, as those who were persecuted under the Jacobin republic now took their revenge against the "ex-terrorists."

The Directorial regime did not, unfortunately, bring stability to France. Elections in 1797 returned a large number of royalists to office. Unwilling to accept that turn to the right, three of the five directors organized a coup, supported by the military, and expelled 177 deputies from office. The following year Jacobins enjoyed a resurgence at the polls, and the directors now refused to tolerate opposition on the left, annulling the election of 121 Jacobin deputies. The government also persecuted political clubs and political newspapers.

In its determination to secure a stable center in French politics, the Directory regime undermined the political process itself, the very motor of the Revolution. The Directory's refusal to tolerate a political opposition had predictable results: not only did fewer voters turn out on election day (since their votes seemed to be worthless), but fewer strong candidates were willing to stand for election. In bringing the Revolution to an end by neutralizing politics, the directors also jeopardized the republic. Unwilling, or unable, to draw its legitimacy from the electorate, the regime had relied increasingly upon the military. It remained only for a strong figure to emerge and take control of this depoliticized government. As before, the directors cooperated in their own undoing by virtually handing power to Napoleon Bonaparte.

The Directory Regime and the Rise of Napolean

The Abbe Sieyès, that firebrand of 1789, played the leading role in the coup that brought Napoleon to power. The war against Europe continued in 1799, and though the French armies had done well in the field, they suffered setbacks in Italy that year. There were economic problems at home as well, in part due to the elimination of the *assignats*, which created a currency shortage. Morale was low, strong leadership needed. Sieyès hoped for a figurehead, someone whom directors like himself could control from behind the scenes. His first choice, General Joubert, inconveniently died on the battlefield. Sieyès and his colleagues turned to Napoleon.

Sieyès and Napoleon launched their coup on 18 Brumaire VIII (November 9, 1799), warning of a dangerous Jacobin conspiracy that threatened to throw the country once again into anarchy and terror. Confronted by this danger, the two legislative bodies held special sessions the following day at St. Cloud, just outside Paris. There Napoleon proposed revision of the constitution to allow his accession to power. Plans went awry, however, when uncooperative deputies protested Napoleon's request and called for his arrest. Ultimately the army ousted dissenters from the meeting hall, in the midst of which Napoleon apparently fainted. The result was the appointment of Napoleon, Sieyès, and Roger-Ducos as consuls. Napoleon soon became First Consul, then First Consul for life, and finally, in 1804, he crowned himself Emperor in Notre-Dame Cathedral. He ruled France until 1815, when his defeat by Wellington's troops at the battle of Waterloo toppled him from power and sent him into permanent exile.

Napoleon's relation to the Revolution is a complicated one. Some who assisted in his rise to power expected him to be faithful to the principles of 1789-91, preserving civil liberties and legal equality within the framework of a constitutional state. This was not just wishful thinking—Napoleon had in fact supported the Jacobins in 1792-93. But in power he adhered more to the policies of the Directory. A new constitution preserved republican forms, but without republican substance. Only the elite were eligible for election to legislative bodies

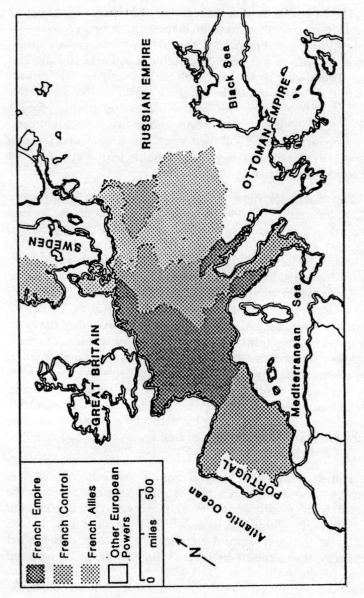

MAP 5: Napoleonic Empire

without any power to initiate legislation. Only the very wealthy were eligible to vote. The new constitution restricted both freedom of assembly and freedom of the press, although the Napoleonic Code preserved legal equality. All were equally subject to the repressive police power of the Napoleonic state.

If Napoleon can be seen as betraying many of the Revolution's ideals at home, beyond France's borders he carried the revolutionary program forward. At the height of its power, in 1810-1812, the Napoleonic empire embraced Spain, Italy, Belgium, the Netherlands, most of the German states, and much of Poland (see Map 5). Scandinavia, Prussia, and the Austrian empire were allied with France at that point. Although Napoleon's disastrous campaign against Russia in 1812 would bring that European domination to an end, in the previous decade Napoleon had undermined feudalism throughout Europe, introduced his legal code in the countries France controlled, fostered notions of representative government, and awakened in those countries occupied by his armies a spirit of nationalism that would be the dominant force in European history for the next century.

LEGACY

The preceding assessment of Napoleon Bonaparte has already suggested certain aspects of the legacy of the French Revolution. As R.R. Palmer has put it, the Revolution quickly escaped the bounds of history and ascended to the status of myth (Chapter 10). The symbols of the Revolution—the fall of the Bastille, the phrygian cap, the guillotine—became enduring symbols that to this day can evoke feelings of awe or terror in the hearts of those who contemplate them. The French Revolution was the first modern revolution, and every revolutionary party since then has studied its history, to be inspired by its achievements and forewarned by its failures. The Jacobin republic was the first modern experiment with democracy, and that experience awakened a new respect for a political system that most European theorists had dismissed as inevitably leading to mob rule and anarchy. The Revolution awakened sentiments of nationalism both within France and throughout Europe, and those sentiments ultimately would bring about the crumbling of monarchical empires and the creation of new nation-states. Liberalism—the ideal of constitutional, representative government—has its roots in the Revolution, particularly in the years 1789-1791. Socialism, too, finds inspiration in the 1790s, though few of the revolutionaries can truly be called socialist. Yet Gracchus Babeuf and his followers did propose redistribution of property in 1795, and workers in the 19th century, convinced that the bourgeoisie had betrayed the common people in the first Revolution, argued that true political equality would come only when economic equality had been achieved. We should note, too, that many see a clear link between the ideals of 1789 and the communist ideal first proposed by Karl Marx and Friedrich Engels.

We see the mixed legacy of the French Revolution very clearly in the subsequent history of Great Britain and Russia. The British at first applauded the revolutionaries in France, convinced that their goal was a constitutional monarchy like their own. The founding of Jacobin corresponding societies in England alarmed the British government, however, and the execution of Louis XVI convinced many of the English that the French had gone too far. Napoleon's dream of empire made the ideological threat from France a very real one for Great Britain, and the enduring legacy of the Revolution across the Channel was an image of anarchical terror on the one hand (the excesses of democracy) and the memory of Napoleonic ambition on the other. Throughout the 19th century the British elite sought to control popular politics through reform and to control France through diplomacy.

In Russia Tsar Alexander I was similarly appalled by the actions of the revolutionary crowd in France, and for the next quarter century he collaborated with the other European monarchs to hold back the revolutionary tide, mostly through repression and not reform. Russia, of course, had played a prominent role in defeating Napoleon. This had two major effects. First, it created a false sense of strength among the Tsar and his advisers, and postponed necessary reforms. Second, the Russian army's march to Paris exposed the officer corps to French civilization and revolutionary ideals. As in so much of the rest of the world, those revolutionary ideals would soon take root even in the monolith of the Russian autocracy. Indeed, it would be in Russia, in 1917, that the next great world revolution would occur.

WORKS CITED

Connelly, Owen, *French Revolution/Napoleonic Era* (New York: Holt, Rinhart & Winston, 1979)

Darnton, Robert, *The Literary Underground of the Old Regime* (Cambridge: Harvard University Press, 1982)

Gendzier, Stephen J., ed., *Denis Diderot's The Encyclopedia: Selections* (New York: Harper & Row, 1969)

Goubert, Pierre, *The Ancien Régime: French Society, 1600–1750*, translated by Steve Cox (New York: Harper & Row, 1969)

Lefebvre, Georges, *The Coming of the French Revolution*, translated by R. R. Palmer (Princeton, NJ: Princeton University Press, 1967)

MacDonald, Joan, *Rousseau and the French Revolution, 1762–1791* (London: 1964)

Miller, James, *Rousseau: Dreamer of Democracy* (New Haven: Yale University Press, 1984)

Palmer, R. R., *The World of the French Revolution* (New York: Harper & Row, 1971)

Tocqueville, Alexis de, *The Old Regime and the French Revolution*, translated by Stuart Gilbert (Garden City, NY: Doubleday, 1955)

Torrey, Norman L., ed., *Les Philosophes: The Philosophers of the Enlightenment and Modern Democracy* (New York: Perigee, 1980)

INDEX

Alexander I, Tsar of Russia 102
Assembly of Notables 54
assignats 72 (illustration), 73, 97
Austria 14, 67, 82–84, 99
Babeuf, Gracchus 101
Bastille 41, 63–64, 90, 101
Beaumarchais 21
Belgium 99
Billaud-Varenne 82, 88
Bourbon 5, 11, 67, 90
bourgeois, bourgeoisie 12, 21–23, 50, 59, 60, 69, 79, 101
Brienne, Loménie de 54
Brissot, Jacques-Pierre 81
cahiers 60–61
calendar 90–91
Calonne, Charles Alexander de 53–54
Capetian dynasty 11
Carolingian dynasty 11
Carrier, Jean-Baptiste 88
Charlemagne 5, 11, 15
chartered towns 17
Church, Roman Catholic 4, 35–37, 47, 53, 70, 72–76

Civil Constitution of the Clergy 74–75
clergy 15, 17, 19, 34–37, 61–62, 67, 69, 77
Colbert, Jean Baptiste 13, 28
Committee of Public Safety 87–88, 93
Committee of General Security 87
Concordat 76
Constituent Assembly 71, 73, 76–78, 81
Constitutional Monarchy 62, 71–79, 89
Copernicus 40–41
Corday, Charlotte 89
Cordeliers 78, 81
corporatism 4, 16–18
Council of State 12, 31–32
counterrevolution 73, 75, 86, 87–88, 93
d'Alembert, Jean le Rond 15, 43–44
Danton, Georges Jacques 79, 82, 85, 87, 88, 93
dérogeance 20
Descartes, René 39
Desmoulins, Camille 62

de-Christianization 76, 88

Diderot, Denis 15, 43–44

Directory 95–96, 97

Edict of Nantes 35

émigrés 81

Encyclopedia 43–45

England 5, 8, 9, 14, 27, 28, 50, 53–54, 66, 84, 87, 102

Enlightenment 4, 39, 46–47, 49, 50, 90

estates 15–16, 37, 54

Estates General 54, 55, 59–60, 62

Federalist revolts 86

feudalism 25, 27, 65, 90, 99

Fronde 11

Galileo 40

German states 99

Girondins 81–82, 83–86, 90

Gouges, Olympe de 79

Grand Alliance 14

Great Fear 64

Great Chain of Being 15

Great Britain
 see England

guilds 16–17, 28, 76

Hébert, Jacques 88, 93

Henri IV 11, 35

hobereaux 20

honor 21

Huguenots 14, 35

Ile de France 5

Intendants 12, 32, 33, 53

Italy 99

Invalides 63

Jacobin Clubs 78–79, 81–82, 84, 85, 88, 90, 93, 97, 102

Jesuit Order 35

Julius Caesar 11

Kant, Immanuel 39

"La Marseillaise" 91

Lafayette 65, 67, 68, 71, 73, 81–82

language 3, 6–7

Law of Suspects 88

Legislative Assembly 77, 81–82

liberty trees 90

lit de justice 33

Locke, John 41

Louis XIII 11

Louis XIV 3–5, 11–14, 19, 20, 31–33, 35, 42, 49, 51, 52, 90

Louis XV 19, 51–52

Louis XVI 11, 19, 51–54, 59, 62, 66–71, 74, 77–78, 81–84, 102

mainmorte 25

Marat, Jean-Paul 83, 85, 89

Marianne 91

Index

Marie Antoinette 62, 67–68, 82, 84

Maupeou 47

Mazarin 11, 12

mercantilist policy 28

Mirabeau, Honoré-Gabriel de 61, 65, 71

Montagnards 83–86

Montesquieu, Charles Louis de Secondat, Baron de 66

municipal revolutions 64

Napoleon 69, 79, 94, 95–99, 102

Napoleonic Civil Code 79

National Assembly 62, 64–69, 78, 91

National Convention 82–87, 93, 95

Necker, Jacques 53, 59, 60, 62–63, 64

Newton, Isaac 40

nobility 13, 15–16, 17, 19–21, 37, 53, 60–61, 62, 67, 68–69, 71, 88

parlementaires 19, 60

parlements 13, 17, 19, 33, 42, 47, 50, 53, 60

pays d'état 5, 17, 32, 33, 53

pays d'élection 5

peasantry 23–25, 27

philosophes 41, 46–47, 79

Phrygian cap 90, 101

Physiocrats 29, 54

Pius VI 74

press 48

Protestants 14, 35, 41

Prussia 14, 83–85, 99

Quesnay, Françoise 28

refractory clergy 74, 82

Revolutionary Tribunal 88

Richelieu 11

Robespierre, Maximilien 78, 81, 85, 87, 88, 91, 93–94, 95

Roger-Ducos 97

Rousseau, Jean-Jacques 44–46, 67, 79, 90

Russia 3, 12, 43, 99, 101–102

Saint-Etienne, Rabaut 60

Saint-Just 84, 87, 93, 95

sans-culottes 69, 90

Scandinavia 99

Scientific Revolution 40

seigneurs, seigneurial system 20, 22, 24, 27, 65, 69

September massacres 83, 85

Seven Years' War 8, 33, 52

Sieyès, Abbé Emmanuel-Joseph 60, 61, 65, 97

taxation 33–34, 52–54, 61, 65, 71, 77

Temples of Reason 76

Tennis Court Oath 62
Terror 87–88, 93–94, 96
tithe 25, 27
trade 8–9, 27–29, 49, 54–55
Tuileries Palace 68, 77, 82, 84
Versailles 3, 12–13, 50, 52, 62, 64–65, 67–69, 89

Voltaire 40, 41–42, 44, 90
War of the Spanish Succession 14
Waterloo 97
Wellington 97
women 23, 50, 68–69, 78–79